Loyal Soldiers

in the

Cocaine Kingdom

Alfredo Molano

Loyal Soldiers

in the

Cocaine Kingdom

Tales of Drugs,

Mules, and Gunmen

TRANSLATED BY JAMES GRAHAM

COLUMBIA
UNIVERSITY
PRESS

NEW YORK

Columbia University Press

Publishers Since 1893

New York   Chichester, West Sussex

Copyright © 2004 Alfredo Molano

Copyright © 2004 Columbia University Press

Library of Congress Cataloging-in-Publication Data
Molano, Alfredo.
  Loyal soldiers in the cocaine kingdom : tales of drugs, mules, and gunmen / Alfredo Molano ;
translated by James Graham.
    p.   cm.
  ISBN 0-231-12914-9 (cloth : alk.paper) —0-231-12915-7 (pbk. : alk.paper)
  1. Drug traffic—Colombia. 2. Narcotics dealers—Colombia. 3. Cocaine industry—
Colombia. I. Title.
HV5840.C7M636   2004
363.45′09861—dc22   2003055720

Columbia University Press books are printed on

permanent and durable acid-free paper.

Printed in the United States of America

c 10 9 8 7 6 5 4 3 2 1
p 10 9 8 7 6 5 4 3 2 1

Contents

ACKNOWLEDGMENTS   VII

TRANSLATOR'S ACKNOWLEDGMENTS   IX

FROM THE MAELSTROM, WITH THEIR COUNTRY ON THEIR BACKS   1
James Graham

The Mule Driver   7

Scuzzball   24

Hanged Man   35

Eight Years, Three Months, One Day   45

Sharon's Diary   69

The Nun   98

Puppet   120

NOTES   155

Acknowledgments

I had heard Ivonne Nichols spoken of in the same way that people speak of a shadow, a perfume, or a battle, until one day Antonio Caballero wrote me about her and I came to the conclusion that she was a woman of flesh and bone. And eyes. At that time she was working at the Columbian Consulate in Madrid and, off the cuff, she suggested I write something about those parts of ourselves living and suffering forgotten in prisons in other countries, whom many of our compatriots would be happy to bury so as not to cause embarrassment at embassy cocktail parties or at the airport.

I also wish to thank the following for the generous and unconditional support that helped make my work possible: José Alejandro Cortés, Augusto López Valencia, María Cristina Mejía, Efraín Forero, Álvaro Escallón, Jackie Goldstein, Nathan Peisack, Edmundo Esquenazi, Teresita Fayad, and Jeanclaude Bessudo.

Translator's Acknowledgments

The translator thanks Silvio Martinez Palau, Christina Chow, Tony Vasquez, and Gudrun Arndt for their assistance, material and spiritual, during the ferocious winter of 2002–3.

From the Maelstrom, with Their Country on Their Backs

JAMES GRAHAM

War is God's way of teaching Americans geography.
Ambrose Bierce, *The Devils' Dictionary*

Colombia is a small country somewhere on the periphery of Latin America, far away from the United States. Full of music, mountains, and troubles of various kinds, it suffers from perennial political difficulties—about which the dominant media in this country tell us precious little—while playing the role of supplier to our drug habit. (Without which, it goes without saying, said habits would not exist.) Long ago it had something to do with the creation of the Panama Canal, but beyond that assertion the rest is hazy or mere history. Countries like Israel, Iraq, and Cuba have made a much larger claim on our consciousness, indeed they have pushed the combined landmass of Colombia, Bolivia, Ecuador, Brazil, Chile, and Argentina off the very edge of the world.

And that, more or less, is Colombia's entry in the psychopolitical glossary Americans carry in their back pockets, a handy all-purpose reference guide (*Details of the Known World*, Washington D.C.: U.S. Government Printing Office, 2003) issued by our rulers and updated semiannually or in case of national emergency.

Needless to say, Colombia exists as a country, with a history and complex reality apart from our willful attempts to ignore it. At the present time Colombians live in the midst of a low-intensity civil war in a country ruled by four powers: the government, the guerrillas, the drug syndicates, and the right-wing paramilitaries. Before the reader dives into this book, it might be worthwhile to take a brief look at Colombia's recent past, to get a feel for where the people in these pages are coming from.

I

On April 9, 1948, shortly after noon near the heart of downtown Bogotá, the populist labor leader Jorge Eliécer Gaitán was shot at close range and killed. Set against the backdrop of the Pan-American Conference presided over by U.S. secretary of state Marshall, no other act could so bring home the reality that the cold war had begun in Latin America. Gaitán's unsolved murder led to days of rioting in Bogotá, which in turn sparked a ten-year, nationwide civil war between Liberals and Conservatives. Incidents like the one described at the beginning of "Hanged Man"—where a villager happens upon a group of Liberals executing Conservatives and gets his neck broken for his trouble— must have been very common on all sides. Three hundred thousand people died in the conflict. In one way or another the civil war—*la violencia* to those who lived through it—touches everyone in this book.[1]

After a decade of violence (roughly '48 to '57), with the furies of slaughter abated, Colombia was perhaps ready to settle its accounts peaceably. But the world is rarely so simple. More than ten years after the death of a charismatic leader and the ensuing struggle for control of the countryside, it was time for the outside world to make itself felt in Colombia.

Cocaine was the drug of choice for gamblers and the Mob who ran the casinos in pre-Revolutionary Cuba, and Colombia—whose pivotal location and far-flung geography have historically provided fertile ground for smugglers—became the distribution point for all South America. After the Cuban Revolution chased the casinos north, Colombians stepped in to run the business, and the modern cocaine trade was born.

A little more than twenty years later, large Colombian cartels were running the cocaine trade as personal fiefdoms, and their wealth and political access led them, during Belisario Betancur's presidency (1984– 1986), to offer to wipe out the national debt in exchange for a promise that the heads of the cartel bosses would not be extradited. An offer that seems to come from a more innocent age, before the days of rampant hostage taking and the armies of street kids who work as paid assassins for a few dollars and a ghetto blaster.

James Graham

On the political front the Colombian left, influenced by the transfigurative events in Cuba, abandoned electoral politics in the 1960s for the dream of revolution. Guerrillas began their long war against the government and, win or lose, have always had the country's enormous landmass to melt back into. By the late sixties the government had imported counterinsurgency tactics with little success and much violence; the countryside was in upheaval but in the cities the status quo was maintained, at least for the rich and powerful. By the late 1990s then President Pastrana found himself offering the guerrillas a reserve approximately the size of Switzerland in which to cool their heels. Or, more accurately, to rearm and plan the next round.[2]

The guerrillas and the drug cartels were two different species with one talent in common: the ability to exploit the power vacuum opened by a weak government. As presidents and administrations have followed one after the other in the last twenty years (1980–2003), the cartels and guerrillas have increased their stranglehold on the country.

While the marijuana crop has moved north to Mexico and ultimately across the border into our backyards, no amount of white powder has been able to slake North America's thirst for cocaine. Drug czars come and go, but every year more and more cocaine makes its way to our shores and up our noses. Even now, with the U.S. government fervently trying to convince the populace that drug use is akin to supporting terrorism, cocaine is more plentiful in North America and the price lower than at any time in memory.

It is exactly in this treacherous environment, in a rapidly changing society unmoored from its traditional values, flush with the drug money that has turned Colombian society upside down, that the people in this book have come of age.

II

Alfredo Molano's vivid firsthand account of Colombians involved in the drug trade is certainly about drugs, but more devastatingly it is about the corner that many Colombians find themselves backed into. They are ordinary people who are drawn to the trade by the question that Perla poses to herself in the chapter titled "Sharon's Diary": "To know once and for all if I get rich or am going to go through my whole life fucked." Most telling about the choices she gives herself is the lack of alternatives: either get with the program or remain a cleaning lady for the rest of your life. There is always petty crime, of course, or one can join the guerrillas, both of which Puppet in Molano's final chapter does for a short while. But, for someone who wants a better life the choices are stark, and the penalties, on both sides of the law, terrible.

So Perla and all the others roll the dice, and a series of events are set in motion from which there is no going back.

As the character known as Scuzzball and others in this book make clear, it's not the Colombians running the risks, processing the raw materials, and transporting it out of the country in their intestines, who are getting rich. It's the big dealers and their syndicates who enjoy the fruit of everyone else's labor.

What's more, the network of police and drug dealers is all too often a single mesh whose goal is to grow rich while simultaneously entrapping as many Colombians as possible. Since no one expects the drug trade to end, it has need of a perennially fresh supply of victims.

From my own particular vantage on the Lower East Side during the roaring, drug-fueled eighties and nineties, I cannot recall a single person I knew who got out alive with any of that "mad money" in their possession. If they did manage to get out alive at all. On the fringes of the drug world people simply disappear at an alarming rate. Closer to the center of power, families and fortunes are chess pieces in a winner-take-all match. Like the snake of legend that consumes its own tail, the trade in illegal drugs eats its own.

What then to make of the personal accounts in this book? Each chapter is a lacerating self-portrait, a confession dipped in acid by a person making bad decisions until things spiral out of control. Betrayal lurks on all sides. After the last false move, the narrator falls into a labyrinth of corrupt police, interrogations, torture, and then prison. Some escape; most do not. Those who do have more luck than wisdom, as the Brazilian proverb has it.

Yet reading this book is like looking at a Colombian Brueghel, a street scene in which the eye moves restlessly from one character to another, each of them adding to the mosaic, a portrait of Colombia in its current impasse. Each individual in this book brings many others with her or him, showing exactly the extent to which drugs infiltrate every level of society until no class or region is left untouched. By letting the people themselves talk and tell their tales, Molano does us a great service: he shows us the people's undiminished energy, despite the obstacles they face and draws a detailed portrait of Colombia in the process.

III

Testimonial literature has its roots in the 1960s. Five years before Studs Terkel's *Hard Times* introduced the genre to American audiences, the poet Roque Dalton sat down in Prague with the legendary Miguel Marmol, a working-class organizer and survivor of El Salvador's bloody 1932 massacre. What were going to be notes for a magazine article turned into a nearly five-hundred-page, stream-of-conscience autobiography by one of the twentieth century's great survivors.[3]

Alfredo Molano Bravo was born in Bogotá in 1944 and is a sociologist, writer, and journalist. His books show a commitment to those people whose voices would not otherwise be heard. It is my feeling that his current exile from Colombia is the price he pays for daring to utter the simple truth that it is the Colombians themselves who are the greatest victims of the drug trade, that they are but game pieces in the long war between the government, the narcs, the guerrillas, and the cartels.

The latest twist in Colombia's fateful encounters with the *Misters* of North America—remembering of course that Teddy Roosevelt felt it was cheaper to create a new country called Panama than to negotiate with the Colombian government of his time—is called Plan Colombia, which happy-go-lucky President Clinton assured us has no political component to it at all. It's just a massive injection of military aid. Nonetheless, as of this writing, U.S. Drug Enforcement Agency planes and helicopters are being shot down over the jungle and sierra at a rate of one every month or so. Their loss goes largely unnoticed while another, more spectacular war bombards the Middle East and the nation's TV screens.

This book makes it clear why Plan Colombia will never succeed: because it ignores culture and history. Because Colombia is not the U.S., ripe for a new Prohibition. Because eliminating the production of cocaine and now heroin will require the elimination of all those Colombians whose aspirations for a better life are frustrated by the current status quo. No military campaign will ever extinguish the narcotics trade, because it would first be necessary to eliminate the disenfranchised members of society, individual by individual.

The people in this book are survivors. They will eventually get out of jail, some with their dignity intact, to be replaced in their cells by other, younger mules and dealers. Yet there is something to the dogged and picaresque spirit of this book's protagonists that gives one hope. If Colombians are indeed passing through an inferno, they do so, as the nun says, with their country on their backs; the fate of their country is no different than their determination to survive. They will endure, she says, "Because, in spite of the blood and the sadness, the sun is still coming up and the people keep on outwitting their misfortunes. The people live, and that's why they kill them. And the more they kill, the more your life recovers strength and meaning."

Despite the tragedy that has befallen the people in this book, despite their bad judgment and their naïveté, there seems reason to believe that the people will ultimately outwit their many relentless pursuers. But what will be left of Colombia after the furies of eradication and punishment have exhausted themselves, no one can say.

This is a small book, the songs of the jailbirds, tales told by those who couldn't shake their demons or solve the riddle of unending poverty. But it is also perhaps the trill of the canary who sings outside the mine before it collapses. Because, it seems safe to say, the present stalemate in Colombia cannot continue indefinitely, especially in light of the massive amounts of military aid pouring into the country.

The question remains, who is listening?

April 9, 2003

James Graham

The Mule Driver

She showed up right on time, arriving in a sweat as if she had just finished a game of basketball. She had long chestnut hair, which she had to cut later for the trip. She came in wearing blue jeans, a yellow sweater, and school girl's tennis shoes. She put the magazine *Cromos* down on the table and asked for a lemon soda. The cafeteria was full of students and employees. She didn't look nervous, although she kept trying to tear off the hangnail on her middle finger with her teeth.

Her name was Lucía and she was studying for her undergraduate degree at the Camilo Torres school. I think, from what they told me, that her boyfriend was serious about her because they were planning to get married. A little later a young black guy, maybe twenty years old, arrived and sat down next to her. He laid *Cromos* down on the table and asked for a lemon soda. They kept coming in one by one until all the mules were there: two young women, a very well-dressed lady, and an older guy. All of them followed the instructions to the letter. I watched them carefully without their knowing it. They didn't even know why it was arranged for them to carry a magazine in their hand and drink a lemon soda. For us it was a test that allowed us to get to know their faces and study their defects. We had to reject the lukewarm, the nervous, the timid, the fearful. Over the course of a full hour I observed them down to the tiniest detail.

Three days later, and in the almost same order that they had arrived at the cafeteria, they got on the airplane. They were spread throughout the seats. None of them knew any of the others and, for sure, none of them knew me, the man who was going to be taking care of them. They didn't seem any more nervous than the other passengers, although each of them carried on average a kilo in their intestines.

When the stewardesses pull the doors shut and it quiets down inside, you feel as if you're halfway to a successful score because you've passed two tests: you've stowed the luggage and been checked by DAS.[1] You know that the police are looking at you and that at any moment they can walk up to a person and say "Come with me." The voyage stops right then and there. When the jet lifts off and you feel it shaking, you know that from that moment you're in another country, where other authorities hold sway, that our poor excuses for cops who can be bought for a thousand or ten thousand pesos are stuck back on the ground. But, in any case, you feel a lot more at ease when the plane picks up velocity and the past gets further behind you, although the cookies remind you who you are. Because you never stop feeling them in your stomach. Women who've had children say that they feel the same nausea at the third month of pregnancy.

There's no other way to do it because there are thirty, forty, or fifty little plastic bags, each of them about the size of a brownie, sitting in your intestines.[2] For sure, the mules are forbidden to eat during the twenty-four hours before the trip, but, in any case, a kilo is a kilo. Some of them take the cookies with Coca-Cola, others with sugar water, and a few just with water. A few try to vomit and others simply can't swallow it at all. Those are the ones who miss the airplane. From early on the mules are checked out one by one with their suitcases, their papers, and their money, all of them ready to get the jump on the job. They pack and go out to the airport, where one person waits for them. In this journey one never flies alone; Madrid is a dangerous place and, for that reason, one person keeps a close eye on the rest.

When the overhead lights go out I take the time to look over their faces again, to figure out where they're all sitting and calm myself down. It was hard work not staring at Lucía, because she struck me as the kind I really like. But love on an airplane is a bad omen. Better, I thought, once we've unloaded I can tell her who I am and confess that I haven't stopped staring at her since the cafeteria. To be a mule driver you have to know how to control yourself and to take every step required. All the mule drivers, every one of them, has been a mule, and they've hit the jackpot more than once.[3]

I made five trips before they gave me the responsibility of taking care of others. In fact, taking care of the merchandise they're carrying and that, in part, is one and the same thing. They pay you when he or she delivers the merchandise in good condition, or, to tell it like it is, when the mules take a crap and then clean the containers with soap and water so they don't smell bad. The hardest parts of the trip are the meals, because you've got to eat a little so that the stewardesses don't catch on to the trick. Almost all of them are spies, although plenty are mules too. Some are spies and mules at the same time, making them spymules. The difference is that they don't carry the merchandise the way we do in our stomachs but inside the walls of the cargo containers that carry their bags or in their powder compacts. They spy in order to gain the trust of the authorities, eliminate competitors, or shake off their bad dreams.

Among the mules there's one of every kind. There are sane people and corrupt people; people who make the journey because they have to and people who do it just for the thrill. I knew a mule from a good family, with a high-sounding last name, who made the trip solely so she could buy nice clothes in Madrid. She was from the coast, tall with big green eyes. Really wicked. She carried a good deal of coke, even for a mule, and traveled in first class. She was scandalous and flirted with whoever was close to her, big or small, old or young, man or woman. They seized her because she arrived on a three-day trip. From the moment she got into the airplane she began to attract attention. Well-dressed, wearing fur and high leather boots. Her boyfriend was very elegant as well, with an overcoat and an executive briefcase. They attracted attention from the time they showed their passports, both of them diplomatic. They drank champagne throughout the flight, and they made a loud, tacky party out of it. They slept for awhile and when they woke up they started asking for champagne. It was a flight to Paris. In Martinique they went out to buy rum and almost didn't make it back. When the plane landed at Orly they had no idea where they had come from or where they had gone. Or where they woke up, because the police seized them for disorderly conduct, and, after going through their suitcases, discovered two kilos. The couple were forced to snap out of their drunkenness, handcuffed to a bed in the airport police station, and were later sent to the Rogny Marigni prison, one of fourteen prisons in Paris, where I ran into them again a year later. She was in the women's section and he in the men's. From a friend I was visiting I learned that they were both rich and they transported the coke just so they could party, dress in the finest clothes, and keep up appearances in their world. They gave the woman five years and the man one, because the merchandise was found in her suitcase.

I also got to know "troubled" mules who made the trip simply out of necessity. Women with five kids abandoned by their husbands. One of them, Doña Tila, was stuck in Carabanchel on account of the "airport," that is to say, she had a kilo in her belly all because she was a widow with three kids. Her husband, a bus driver in Bogotá, was killed so they could get their hands on the day's proceeds. One night around nine he parked the bus in the lot as usual, got out, said goodnight to the watchman, and headed home. When he got to the corner the robbers jumped him, and they left him there spilling blood. She nearly went mad, but with three little kids it was her job to keep things together and look for a way out. She found it. She got involved with a con man who introduced her to the job. In one trip, if things go well, they pay between two and three thousand dollars, depending on the deal you've made. Because all of us aren't equal. Doña Tila paid her dues because she had to, and so they only promised her fifteen hundred. They gave her five hundred in the airport and another five in Madrid. The balance would be paid when she returned to Bogotá. The business is conducted that way so that the worker goes back, and since they aren't carrying money in their pockets there's no reason for them to get out of line because they're closely watched and observed. Very few mules make more than two trips.

They aren't allowed to find out much about the workings of the business because they'll get up to speed and take off to start their own line. For security reasons the individual mules don't know their companions on the trip or the rendezvous where they arrive. Security is security for the merchandise. The mules know all that they need to know in order to crap out the product in good condition and to come back for their money, which is waiting for them in cash.

Doña Tila was a woman from way out in the sticks. She ate everything they gave her on the plane and even asked for more. She'd never flown before and she thought that the plastic bags were tucked away who knows where. The result was, they asked her where she was going and, in spite of being told many times what her answers should be, she couldn't do it, she was too excited and didn't say a word. They asked her how much she was carrying, she took out her five hundred dollars—which for her was all the money she'd ever seen in her life—and, definitely the guards were suspicious, they inspected her and forced her to get rid of the cookies. And then, what a sharpie she was, she told everything she knew; which was all they needed to put her behind bars on her own. In Carabanchel she threw herself into working in every part of the prison and from that she was able to support her kids in Bogotá. When her sentence was up she didn't want to leave the prison because she knew that in Colombia she wasn't going to find anything to help her finish raising her little sardines, who were already in college.

That time we arrived in Madrid without a hitch. There are two big steps, which are the heavy ones. The first is when you exit the plane and you walk down a long corridor, where they look everyone up and down and take in all the details: comportment, relaxation, uneasiness, your clothes, how you look. From there the candidates go to the second step, where they present their papers. This is the place where the guard comes up to one of the mules and says, "Come with me to be searched." And they already know: eight years, three months, one day. But Lucía passed through without any trouble, her eyes as dead as a flattened mosquito. All the mules made it through, the whole bunch, and on the way out of Barajas each one, unaware of the others, took a taxi for the hotel, which that time was the Rey de Bastos.

I couldn't restrain myself and went up to Lucía on the way out of the airport. I didn't ask her anything more than whether she was going to the Rey de Bastos, but she felt she'd been caught. I calmed her down and, so that she'd open up quickly, told her I was taking care of her. We are forbidden to let anyone know who we are for fear of being caught, but I'd fallen in love with the girl; she was so delicate, so innocent, and I fell into the trap of telling her who I was. I knew she needed help getting to the hotel. Anybody knows that a mule feels extremely lost, like an orphan, after nine hours on the plane, having endured fear and badly digested hopes, and then they arrive at a building where no one is waiting for them. She thanked me for the hand I held out to her and accepted my help. I left her in the hotel after having checked that every one of my "charges" was in their proper room. I called them by phone from the corner to give them instructions: "Get the cookies out, clean them carefully, count and package them for Arturo to come by to collect them. I'll call you back in half an hour to find out if there are any problems." Sometimes Lotomil, which they take so that they won't shit during the flight, works too well and they have to drink castor oil so they can dump the bags out. It happens to one out of every five.

While my mules were sleeping and resting up I went to talk to Saul, a Colombian who lived near the Puerto de Sol, telling him that the merchandise had already arrived so he could send for it to be picked up. That was my job. At night, when all of it had been collected and weighed and everything was in order, I pounced on Lucía. We went out partying from bar to bar in La Castellana, pouring the party out of bottles of Chinchón, the only aguardiente something like our own. We partied until the sun came up and we woke up together. And we woke up together the next day and the next day after that, until one night I realized that I'd fallen in love and so, for professional reasons, I left her and went back to Bogotá to prepare for the next shipment. I held out for fifteen days, and, on the next shipment, she was back again, her eyes assaulting me. She was even prettier than the first time. I changed seats with the man who was sitting next to her and we arrived together in Madrid bewitched from loving each other so much.

With Lucía life paid back a debt. I started working in this line because Virginia, my first girlfriend, left me for someone with money. She was the daughter of a spoiled and corrupt old lady who trafficked in women. She had a house in the Santafé district, where she brought her own daughter's girl friends from school, filled them up with promises, and then shoved them off to Cartagena, where they were at the service of the cruise boats that arrived from Canada loaded down with the monkeys in heat who came to do their thing in the Caribbean sun. Virginia knew about the business but she wanted to study to become a lawyer. I got to know her when I was working at the twenty-four-hour liquor store making deliveries on a motorbike. I met her the afternoon she came to shoot baskets in the park. She was the captain of one of the few women's nonprofessional soccer teams around; she wore an all-white uniform with a red stripe across the chest. She looked cute covered with sweat, and I invited her to take a spin with me on the motorbike and have a milk shake. She said yes and we became friends. I was in love with her, and for every delivery that I made I made an apology for racing off to feel her pussy. Each delivery was a visit. At night I honked the horn for her and kept going. The thing was, two trips for every delivery wore me down; and, instead of making twenty each day, which was the average if you wanted to keep the motorbike, I started to dip under fifteen and, finally, ten deliveries. So they took the keys for the motorbike away and fired me.

My brother, seeing me suffering because I lost the job at the liquor store and, indirectly, the girl, just about kicked me—or, more accurately, my ass. He told me not to be a jerk, why should I have a "job" that had me stooping to work at the beck and call of a boss, killing myself for a lousy salary that would never compensate me. He dragged me off to the Sabana Station for a drink, and, in the middle of knocking them back, I remember him asking me, "Do you want to take long trips? Would you like to taste and live the good life? Alright then, I'm going to introduce you to a man who can get you out of your hole and bring your woman back—and not just that runt you're running with. This dude will hook you up with all the babes in the world. Stop crying and don't be a big jerk!"

On the day that I showed up to be loaded with plastic baggies, that day, at the same hour—four in the afternoon—they were killing my brother at 100th Street and Fifth. They had tipped him off about it. This was a dude who was in the army reserve, a legend among the sharpshooters, he used guns since he was a kid. It was his passion. In

El Dorado he did business with a police captain, they had a total falling out over a shipment, and that son of a bitch became my brother's enemy. He had to kill him. They hunted him down without giving him time to catch his breath and killed him as if he were a common criminal.

I don't know how I managed to keep those cookies inside my gut. At first you feel them moving and they make you want to vomit; then you feel how heavy they are, and you're thirsty. But you know that what you're carrying is closely tied to your destiny. From the moment that you wash them down you depend on them. If the rubber tears, you'll live a few hours; if they don't break but the police seize you, you'll spend eight years of your life behind bars; if you carry it off, you've laid the first layer of bricks that goes toward building a wall between you and poverty. I am a steadfast devotee of the Niño of the twentieth of July, and I know that he helped me to make the trip successfully the five times I carried merchandise inside my stomach.

The group that I was working with gave me permission to have Virginia come along. She wasn't carrying either powder or leaf. If you're carrying, that's OK; but if your woman gets caught up in that web of spiders, judges, and lawyers, it's a lack of respect for her. I rented an apartment in Madrid, and we let her family believe that she had won a scholarship to study modeling. At that time I left off carrying the cookies so I could become a mule driver, and. finally, after making myself a trusted man in the business, I got to know Madrid and went all over Spain, dedicating myself wholeheartedly to moving the merchandise that arrived here. I rented a nice apartment in La Puerta de Oro, and Virginia invited her mother to spend her vacation with us. The mule drivers alerted me when a shipment arrived, and I went to the hotels, got hold of the merchandise, and put it into circulation. I began to manage the "sugar grinders," the little guys who sold to individuals. A really fucked up group, very tricky, very dangerous. I had to keep those dudes away from each other at gunpoint. But everything went well.

I kept my love affair going with Lucía. I loved her tiny body and the nipples on her small breasts, always stiff and alert, as if they were antennas. Virginia didn't realize what was going on because my love affair with Lucía was concealed inside the secret activities of smuggling. Even so, with Lucía I couldn't lie about Virginia because Virginia moved about as plain as day. Many times it occurred to me that I didn't depend on Virginia as much as I did on Lucía. I was wrong, because Virginia's bitch of a mother found out about Lucía and threw the dogs on me. So that I wouldn't find out the game she was playing, she invited her daughter to Miami, and when they walked out the door of the apartment the police busted in on me. The Niño of July 20 protected me, because I had just sent a package with four kilos off to Holland and I only had a few grams, more or less my personal stash, and in Spain they don't mess with you for small amounts. Anyhow, the quantity was enough to go from Plaza de Castilla to Carabanchel.[4] Which I did. Lucía stepped up to handle my case, she sold what she could and paid for a Spanish lawyer who got me out but who left me without five pesetas to my name. I was in for seven months. Lucía kept the business going. ▓

I don't know how it happened, I never understood it, but one Sunday Virginia showed up at the visitor's room instead of Lucía. It was only a few days before I got out, and from that day she went back to holding the reins of my business. I threw out Lucía, threatening to inform on her, and it looked as though there were no repercussions. I let myself fall into Virginia's arms once again. Without a protest. Lucía, in any case, kept working in Madrid.

Having paid my debt the hard way, I returned to the business. I recovered my prestige very quickly, retook the controls, pulled the strings, made contacts, and—the best part—managed the accounts. The little mules brought me all the merchandise I needed, and I took out the part that Madrid consumed, then the part they sucked up in Barcelona, and then the stuff they were begging for in Sevilla. It wasn't enough. The greenhorns had given up on hashish and horse to get deeply involved with a more serious product, which is what the little parakeet is.[5] The blessed mother of them all. Thanks to her I bought a car and an apartment and spent my vacations in Ibiza. Virginia was happy. The risk factor keeps diminishing as you gain responsibility and climb to higher positions in the business. The stairway of power. But everyone always forgets that the fall from the heights hurts more and is more dangerous. Everything balances out in life.

I left the management of the mules in Virginia's hands. I had made it utterly clear to her that I would go to hell with her, but with her mother I wouldn't go even to heaven. We agreed on that, and she stopped calling her on the phone or even mentioning her. Her behavior made me feel so secure and she showed me such great respect that I didn't get involved with the old bitch. It was practically her business, and she went so far as to take it upon herself to make changes in the way things were done, no longer working with men. The line was all women. They came and went, seduced the guards and the police, were on their way and passed without a hitch. Very few were caught. The strangest incident she had to deal with was of a young woman who arrived fully loaded and couldn't let them go. We gave her every possible pill, we cleaned her out with every medicine we knew, and nothing happened. Those cookies seemed to be lodged inside her, as if in a cave. The woman was weeping from the pain and in her anxiety wanted to go back to Colombia because in Spain we couldn't find a surgeon we could trust to operate on her and in any case if she was going to die she would die in her country. The young woman kicked the bucket on the plane going back without saying a word. All the officials at the airport—so they told us—were banging their heads on the wall trying to understand how it was that she was carrying cocaine from Spain to Colombia. We were lucky that we had managed to get her back, because cases like that are very difficult. There's a story from before my time that the bags burst in a mule when she landed in Spain and they couldn't seem to pull them out. The woman died in the hotel, and they didn't have a clue what to do with her body. It was summertime, when everything that isn't in the fridge spoils, and, to make matters worse, the nights are short. The way they tell it, they took her out on a stretcher as if she were sick, put her in a car, cut off her fingers so she couldn't be identified, and threw her into the river with her guts cut open, not only so they could remove what she was carrying but also so the body would sink more rapidly. There are misfortunes that take place, you have to let go and forget about them, because you can't keep turning them over in your mind until the incident poisons you and you end up one of the insane.

I dedicated myself full-time to moving the stuff that came from down south, from our country. We were moving tons and not grams. It came in by way of the Azores in Galician fishing boats and docked on that cold and wretched northern coast. A fellow Colombian—a bit cruel and not in the habit of making friends—ran the line and he kept me busy, because I knew how to keep moving and sell the stuff without wasting a gram. We had a Bolivian coworker, a high-level employee of an English lord who supplied the money in the bargain. The problem was how to handle this pile of cash. With such a quantity given in advance, handling the powder, the little bird, ceases to be the problem, leaving that honor to the bills themselves. To count millions of pesetas takes some doing. I had to weigh the bills, because there isn't enough saliva or time to arrive at a total of how much money there is filling up a bathroom, to name one example. And to move this mountain of bills from one place to another is more difficult than moving the merchandise in powder form. Money is more slippery than powder. It went on the road to Switzerland and, with the lord's help, we sent it back to Colombia because that's where it was born. They invested the money here, and even I myself ended up sinking my earnings into a hotel chain in Bilbao. But you dream about flashing your money in Colombia, your country, where the prestige counts. Here you are taken for a rich guy, but outside the country you're Mr. Nobody. In a place where no one knows you from Adam it's worth it if they look up to you. The mere desire for money ends when you have a lot of it, and the crucial thing is the jealousy it awakens. That's why you long to enjoy the things you have up here back down there. That's what I was thinking. Virginia knew it and she feared its coming, because that put the scenario she was organizing in danger.

Just like that the police got me one morning. She had gone out to the airport and I was alone, in slippers. The cops let me put on my pants and, without being able to alert anyone, I fell into the deep hole that I had leapt out of so many times. Nevertheless, I trusted her, trusted that she had gone out to "do an airport," trusted that she would realize what was up once she left the mules in their hotel. My journey to the jail at Plaza de Castilla was at once too quick and too slow. We went through all the streets, past the street corners and plazas that belonged to me because of all the hairy scenes I'd gone through and all the things I'd done on them. I looked out at the people from the police car I was traveling in and I had gone a few inches, but in reality I was passing through the whole world, the world of liberty. To depend on others, to be under their authority, at the mercy of their will and their whims, you become a minor once again, a forgotten child who can't recognize himself. Memories of the house where I grew up, my parents, my brothers, school, all mixed together with what was happening to me, with the entrance to the Plaza de Castillo, the interrogation, my declaration of innocence, everything that was happening at a terrifying speed. I had never realized how much responsibility rests on what you say, the power and value of each word. Each sentence went in my dossier, and the dossier became the essential key of my future. I fortified myself by thinking that when Virginia returned from the airport she would realize what was happening, she would call a lawyer and see to getting me out shortly after. The reality was that I didn't have anything in the house. I wasn't used to protecting anything that belonged to me. Neither silver nor powder. We had some hundred-eighty grams in the closet, as well as about sixteen hundred dollars: twenty months in the worst case. I followed her in my head from the airport to the hotel, from the hotel to the Plaza de Sol and later to the apartment, while I arrived at the Plaza de Castilla, where they threw me in a cell, booked me, and gave me permission to make one call. At that moment I calculated—as I was doing it, I was getting more and more upset—that she was already in the house and had figured out that something happened to me because the car was still in the garage and I didn't go out to the street on foot. I dialed slowly, slowly, as if giving her time. The noise of the telephone sounded normal, the numbers spun around until the line went through. "Girl," I was going to say. "I'm in jail. A tough mistake; who knows who they're confusing me with. So, Your Majesty, call the lawyer and tell him that a great injustice is being committed, that he needs to clear it up right away. You know what to do to pay him." That's how I was thinking, but nobody answered and the cop told me, "Okay, buddy, time's up; nobody escapes the hooks they have in you."

And that's how it was, nobody picked up the phone. I asked permission for a second call and dialed Lucía's number. She answered. I told her that I had been taken prisoner by mistake and that she should call a lawyer. "Yes," she answered me, "I already know that's what I have to do. Do you remember how you got rid of me, how you robbed me? Do you remember how you exploited me, the son of a bitch that you were to me? Do you remember the way you tricked me? How you treated me like a mule making money for you and like a girlfriend using me up? Do you remember all of it? OK then. Rot in jail, because I was the one who handed you over and not only to the law but to Virginia as well. Virginia is involved in everything; from the airport she left for Columbia. Son of a bitch, rot in that cell. I hope the dampness and the cold kill you. Now you'll pay for the way you robbed us. It's all over. Over," and then click, click. My life split in two. I stood there frozen, as if I didn't know how to get out of the booth. They dragged me out yelling and weeping. My interrogator said to me, "Your women have dumped you here for twenty-five years. You don't have much time left to live. Pull yourself together!"

Everything took place in leaps and bounds, very quickly, as if it was happening to someone else and not me. I was like a puppet on a string who did and said things without knowing who I was. As if I occupied another person who made statements, lied, accused, gave up, and at the end walked into the seventh block of Carabanchel, where they locked me into a cell and condemned me to, sure enough, twenty-six years. Would I be the same person who was born, nursed, grew and became a man, he who was sitting there on his cot, weeping and moaning, calling himself Ancízar and answering to number 3376? I went around in mourning until a smile cut it off with a clean stroke. Then I would sleep until I jumped out of the cot, as if a horsefly had bitten me. I didn't eat. Or I ate very little. I went on living who knows why or what for. But day by day the mourning diminished and turned into anger. Anger and hatred flooded and then poisoned me.

One day I woke up knowing what lay ahead of me. I washed out my eyes, cleaned my face, and went out to take care of life, to play the game exactly as they were playing it with me. A month had gone by already. The prison lawyer helped me to get in touch with my lawyer and to contact my Spanish partners, who told me what I needed to know: "Your properties have been seized by the law; your money is in their hands." At this point all that was left was the deposit that the Bolivian agent managed. With this I began to pay the lawyer, a rat who was selling me dreams named after items in the legal code, lies named after the numbers given to laws. Hopes and more hopes. More corrupt than a cop or a judge, sicker than a drug trafficker, a thief, or a killer, is the lawyer who gets rich at the price of handling your punishment. This son of a bitch, maybe he'd gone to the University of Salamanca, he was stuffed full of titles and affected speech, and he was fleecing me one dollar after another for requests, demands, appeals, and rejoinders, all coming out of the money the Bolivian held for me, but in the end I was stuck doing a solid twenty-two years.

The memory of Virginia tormented me as much as that of Lucía. It didn't let me alone day or night. The story of Lucia's hatred has to begin when, instead of paying a small-time mule named Jacinto, I took his money to pay someone else. It wasn't going to kill him, but the son of a bitch took it like it would. This Jacinto had a crush on Lucía; I knew it, and I dealt with it, because at the end of the day she was my girlfriend and if I wanted her to be just for me, I would have to take care of her. It wasn't easy because Virginia was familiar with the whole system. She knew where and how much money we had, where the accounts were, in which banks, she knew the connections, the chains of command, everything. I'm sure that Jacinto poisoned Lucía until she was so full of venom she went looking for Virginia, told her about the love affair we were keeping hidden, and all the rest. From that moment things happened on their own, as if managed by the Devil himself. She thought it all up, planned it while I went about my business untouched, innocent, making connections. We were sleeping

The Mule Driver

together and I was in love with her; she knew how to get so far inside me she reached that interior only she had seen. I knew that I loved Virginia more, because after having sex with her I kept loving her; this didn't happen with Lucía anymore, because after making love to her I had the urge to throw her dead body right into the garbage. She must have gone about keeping that contempt right there between her thighs, or between her chest and her back, until it had become a mother lode of hatred.

How Virginia must have relished everything that was happening to me, taking pleasure in my punishment and at the same time enjoying my money; enjoying all that which I had created with so much hard work, suffering, and, above all, while putting up with so much fear. That line about money that you hear in the trade, that bringing the greenhorns the stuff they like so much not being work is a big lie. To carry cookies or load a boat full, to get through customs, to take off from the airports is suffering of a kind nobody can imagine. Each person with whom you make connections—and let's not talk about cops but civilians—is or can be an enemy and every one of your friends in the line can be an informer. That's why you go about your business completely devoid of feelings: you know that anyone can sell it and, if you had to, you can sell to anyone. In the drug business loyalties are like money. The one you can trust with the money you can trust with the business and with the people who work for it. But a person who hoards and guards his money isn't trustworthy, you don't have confidence in him and you fear he may take off. Money makes a lot of us happy and we enjoy it when we get it. So, in the business, we're solid and we trust each other.

Virginia was dead and buried inside of me. I found a job in my cellblock, something to do so I didn't go crazy crushing memories. They put me in charge of maintaining cleanliness and hygiene in a pavilion 80 percent Colombian, where many of us knew each other from outside. Some of them had worked with me; they knew who I was and they did what I told them. I had respect because they knew that I never made up stories, I wasn't a punk, that what I did, I really did do; I looked them in their eye so that they would know who I was and what I wanted, so that they would know I was serious. More than once I had to put my life on the line in El Tigre, until people knew who I was.[6]

I didn't want it that way, but Virginia became a monster who consumed the little bit of soul I had left. Without wanting to, without thinking about it, I began to make a plan of how I would make her pay, how she would pay with her life for that which I was paying with my liberty. It was a horrible idea, but I couldn't get it out of my head, I couldn't even hide it. Vengeance was growing all by itself, and merely from thinking about those who made off with my money and with who knows who.

I remembered a young dude, a con man, who lived in Armenia and was my brother's friend. A screwed up kid, very faithful to us and our name. I called him in one of those personal calls that they allow us, I talked to him as plainly as I could, and he, like the good dog that he is, understood everything. It wasn't more than giving him the information so he could start to work, locating her, following her around. She lived with her brother-in-law and she managed all of my business in league with her mother, who kept up her long-time business. I was feeding my decision with hatred, looking for a way to pay the mad gunman. He agreed to do the job in exchange for some gems they owed me and it was his job to get his hands on. At the moment of truth I was in his hands, because the scoundrel could do one thing without doing the other. Everything depended upon the respect that he had for the memory of my brother.

I couldn't go back to sleep waiting for the outcome of the story that I had put together, waiting for Virginia's demise. It was hatred as much as love for that woman, who wasn't alive for me anymore. I made short work of the job, watching the same movie over and over again. My man in Bogotá stalked her, he know the itinerary, the roads, the schedule, her clothes, her friends, and he started to set the trap. I thought that the easiest way to do it was to shoot her and her brother-in-law as they came out of the house that I had purchased the deed to, thanks to a shipment we had brought to La Coruña and, after repackaging, had successfully delivered to New York via Montreal. A house as big as an office building. I sat down on my cot to treat myself to fear and satisfaction. That's the way vengeance is, a pleasurable feeling that caresses you and, caressing you, wraps you up in fear. The thing you don't realize is that the person vengeance destroys is you.

Things turned out the worst way possible. When everything was in place and ready to go, she and her brother-in-law disappeared. Someone dragged them out of the house at dawn, put them in a car, and drove them to the hillsides of Subachoque. They were found murdered, their bodies burned, with a coup de grâce in each of their foreheads. They were killed with a pistol that my brother had left me in his will when he died, a Luger dipped in silver that I never used and that I will never know who used to kill her and her brother-in-law.

The pistol is the only clue I have that keeps me from going crazy now, so I know that it wasn't me who killed them. The gun was in Virginia's hands, she took it along with all my possessions. My con man couldn't have known of its existence, and, therefore, he couldn't have killed them. They must have run up other debts that were collected before mine. Somebody got there first.

Over the course of an entire year I paid for the crime in my head, weeping for the woman on many nights. I loved her. When I learned about the pistol, the sin fell from the altar where it was sitting. I gave up suffering for the crime to begin weeping for her death, paying with the weight of my bad conscience for the crime I wanted to commit but didn't. She, Virginia, now rules over the walls and doorways of this prison that I built with the desire and the urge to kill her.

Scuzzball

Nearly 400 of us are inmates at the prison called Cochabamba Municipal, along with 120 women and 180 children. We are a family, and, as in every family, we respect each other and respect ourselves. The act for which you are condemned, justly or not, doesn't mean that they can treat you like an old mop, any way at all, throwing away the rights that we have as human beings like a piece of paper. It happens that there are disagreements and quarrels between us, but that doesn't mean the authorities can mess with anyone anywhere they like. No. Perhaps being a prisoner is a crime? No. The crime was committed before, the crime stayed on the outside, and that's why you're inside.

Don't think that what we have today is a gift, nor was it decent people who gave it to us. It was up to us to get it for ourselves, fighting inch by inch, day by day. At first, when I arrived, this prison was a hell behind closed walls. There was no rule of law here because the law was imposed by whoever made it. The guards took bribes for everything. To let you in or to let you out, to take the sun in the patio, to work or not to work, to take a piss at night, to make love to your girlfriend, to sell food or to buy it. The guards took bribes from us and the warden took bribes from the guards. It was up to us to fight back the day they let a criminal slip in the jail looking for me under my real name. The scoundrel got in by paying to get here, he walked around until he found me, and if I hadn't pinched myself on the double the dude would have killed me because he came with his shovel raised. I was able to get the jump on him, thanks to a shank the king had loaned me, and I sent the thug to the hospital, where they say that he was just short of dead.

I protested. How is it they let the son of a bitch get in here with his crazy face, dirty, armed, carrying drugs and smelling of booze, without even asking where he was going or what he wanted? At that time I already had a following among the people, and they respected me. Not an easy thing, because the same day they threw me like a dog into the cells of the general population, where thirty of us had to sleep in forty square feet. It was up to me to run after the boss, who controlled things in the cellblock. His name was Rintintin, and he went around wearing a necklace with little bells on it that let people know he was about to arrive, so that they would wait for him like a king. But since we Colombians don't grovel before authority that doesn't earn it the hard way, I had to follow him all around the prison until he let himself be caught in one of the bathrooms where I showed him that I wasn't there on vacation and that if someone was in command it had to be with my permission. That was my opening. I spared his life so that he would give in to me, because if I had knocked him over I would have had to pay for it and dispel doubts in the bargain. Alive I was able to gain the control that he had.

Another time I had to stand up to a gang from Santacruz de la Sierra who arrived after I had gotten settled, bought a cell for a thousand dollars, and had my group established. Fame and reputation assured. It was the Maldiren brothers' gang, half Argentine, half Bolivian, half Paraguayan, half Brazilian. Seven mule drivers who worked in the south, that is to say, those whose job it was to open markets down below, because we Colombians were, and are, in the north. They made a lot of noise when they arrived. I watched them from the king's cell, the only one that has its own bathroom and that's worth six thousand bucks. I said to him, "Don Rey, take a look and see if you know them." He told me, "Sure I do. They're southerners, nobodies and so-and-sos, all right when they're together but cowards on their own. They were ratted out on a shipment they made to Chile; they're also wanted in Los Angeles. It seems to me that they want to make trouble for you because they're going about telling the story that your crew gave them up."

I didn't believe it, because we Colombians are smugglers but not traitors. But I put myself on guard just in case. With Carlos, a guy from Antoquia who is absolutely fearless, I went to their cell one afternoon, when the guards were making the list, or, in other words, taking the head count. It was better to pay for a lack of discipline than to let ourselves be surprised by the Maldiren. So there we were: we swiped their knives, took them for ourselves, and stood our ground while they counted heads. When they had counted and recounted and told everyone to sit on their cots, Carlos and I attacked. They looked for their shanks, but "while the shrimp slept, the tide carried them off." No rewards for good omens. When they reached for their weapons, we were the ones who pulled them out. Three Maldiren to the infirmary and two to the hospital.

From then on Don Rey, who ruled the jail's courtyard, without saying as much, accepted me as the enforcer. Without a word we recognized each other as the powers that be, because an agreement to respect each other was more convenient for both of us than fighting it out to settle things. Between the two of us we shared power, and any third parties that tried to move in we destroyed the first move they made. The other route—if one of us had attacked the other—it would have been very possible that a second would step up to move into command, taking power from the one who went down. Simple psychology. Sharing power between the two of us, we watched each other's back.

That was the way we were able to impose order. The day I sent the con man who came in to kill me packing, that day the people, every one of them, rose up to demand their rights. If the guards were letting anyone and their brother walk on in, nobody was safe inside. The guards took out their sticks and threatened us, above all me, because they knew where the uprising had gotten its start. The inmates were backing us up even when some of us stuck on one side and some on the other. Blocking the door, the guards supported by the police; on the other side us, all of us, even the Maldiren. The guards shouted at us: "Give up!" and then they fired one canister of gas after another. But nothing happened, we didn't give way and the only thing we asked for, at the top of our lungs—the women and children too—was that the warden make an appearance accompanied by the prison's legal adviser. They arrived one right behind the other and thereby avoided a melee, which would have spilled a good deal of blood.

Scuzzball

With the authorities present, we set about demanding that, before anything else, they provide for our safety. No letting anyone in without our permission. The struggle was short because reason was on our side, but where the finger enters the hand follows and gets in: we demanded that women, children, and old people be able to go to the bathroom at night without permission, because in the permission is the bribe; that women be able to go to work in the morning and return in the afternoon; the children be able to go to school and to come to sleep with us; that they no longer charge us for the installation of TV antennas; that they let us build a library, a room to watch movies, and a gymnasium; that they let our lawyers enter when they wanted to; that the Indians be able to chew coca; that the solitary cells be clean. We finished off by saying, "We have to pay for the sins we committed, but don't believe that because of this we have stopped being human beings. Watch where you're walking, don't let the snake bite you."

Don Rey backed me up point by point. The old dude is a refined fellow. He's well known in Santacruz and more than anywhere else in El Beni, where he has haciendas with livestock. He was very rich before getting involved in drug trafficking with General Balsas. The general gave him confidence and together they loaded a plane with three thousand kilos each week. The general had opened his own route from El Beni so that the kilos would be taken on the flight headed to the Yarí plains, straight to Cali and Medellín. At first they used a Bolivian Air Force plane and then later a Turbo 1000 they bought and registered with a license number from another plane that was always parked in Cochabamba, so that the big one was passed off as a tiny plane that wouldn't even harm a fly. In Bolivia, you see, wealthy people have gotten involved in drugs; but in Colombia it's we nameless people who moved it, until those with the nice last names started to ask us for help and little by little we gave it to them, and eventually we take them as partners in the business. That's why the country is going the way it's going.

Don Rey, without getting out of the easy chair that his guards carried for him up and down the stairs—the guy was way heavy and anything tired him out—butted in to say that our cause was righteous and he therefore proposed that we choose a council of delegates to assist in the management of the prison house. No one was opposed. The legal adviser said he had no grounds for opposition and the warden gave in without any objections. Right then and there we chose the delegations: discipline, cleanliness, library, permissions, family, recreation; thirteen delegations in all. We brought out some ballot boxes and each and every one of us voted in secret for whomever we wanted. One of the most straightforward elections I've ever seen. Without last minute changes or tricks we selected the council, and we tied ourselves to the guards so they couldn't continue to rip us off in our position. We showed them that we were a hard and even prickly bone to gnaw on.

Today the prison is the cleanest and safest in the world. If there is no justice outside, we've demonstrated that here inside there is, with no one abusing anyone else. The solitary cell is finished, what I mean is no one has visited it for a long time because there's no need to; there are no shaved heads because no one gets out of line; the fifteen hundred dollars the warden swindled every month is a thing of the past, as is the five thousand that went to the guards. Now we pay for our crimes but we don't pay those who imprison us. If outside the prison they have justice intimidated, here we welcome it and defend it.

I've paid six years of hard time here, four concurrently and two from the prison court. I still have seven left, which I can reduce to two if I work a little bit. I had twenty five years, because they sentenced me for the crime of felony murder in the person of a police officer, one of those dogs who watches over us and who fell in love with my wife. She told me everything from the outset and I let the business take its course until a day that I was pissed off on account of a connection going badly and I decided to take it out on him. I prepared my getaway, I went out, I looked for him, and I killed him in legitimate defense of my honor, as the Superior Court recognized later when I appealed. It's my feeling that at the moment of truth they admitted it because the only crime they associate with Colombians is drug trafficking. ▓

I arrived in Bolivia on February 28, 1991. I came from my house in La Hormiga, Putamayo, where twenty-eight years earlier I was born. My father comes from Pasto and my mother from Campoalegre, Huila; I left them when I was thirteen years old because there's no life where we were living and it was time for me to go looking for it. I was a leaf scraper in the place they call Piñuña Negra, until I learned chemistry. I worked in El Caquetá, in El Guaviare, and finally in El Cauca. I was extracting the merchandise at 90 percent, and when it didn't rain so much I stretched it to 95 percent. I was very well-known as a chemist. In Leticia I learned how to crystallize too and I got to the point of taking out 101 percent. That is to say, for every kilo of simple paste I take out one kilo, ten grams.[1] I consider myself famous for this skill and what I possess I owe to the craftwork I know how to do. From Leticia I set out for Tingo María; the one thing a young guy desires most is to get around, and when you are stuck in a kitchen mixing compounds you see very little of the world.

I went a few days without work, staring at the birds. I left Tingo for Sarapoto and came back without hooking up with anyone. In Sarapoto I used my head to get a job. The Indians were experts at cultivating coca, among other things, because they didn't know how to do anything—or very little—else. But they didn't process it. I also traveled to El Chapare in Bolivia and the whole region with the same plan: looking around and picking up knowledge.

The Peruvians were extracting a damp paste at 70 percent, but they didn't know about the base. They didn't know how to oxidize the merchandise to remove the impurities. They thickened it with kerosene, and the taffy that is left over is no good to work with. I studied the subject and set myself to extracting base for several months until I became bored making money. I extracted, by my calculations, more than a hundred twenty thousand kilos working this way. I teamed up with a few other Colombians and we loaded the heavily packed merchandise onto a plane near Villavicencio. Just the same, I left that job and became a professor. I dedicated myself to teaching how to extract the base, selling my knowledge and the laboratory skills I had developed. I made a lot of money, but, by the same token, I had to watch out for myself, and it cost me a few fistfights to be able to offer my services. More than once my fists had to stick up for me because there was jealousy on all sides. I gave courses of one, two, and three weeks, charging every student five thousand dollars. So by the end of a year I was rich but surrounded by enemies. The bravest ones were my fellow Colombians, because they were living off the laboratories and I was teaching them secrets that I had discovered on my own.

One time we made a shipment of a thousand kilos of hard, shiny crystal. The Turbo Commander arrived at the set hour, and we were taking off when the law showed up. Soldiers everywhere like ants, armed up to their necks. They surrounded us and dumped us with everything and the merchandise onto the same plane. The pilot, a hothead from Antioquia, and I went on first; behind us, a captain and sergeant sticking their R-15s in our backs. We took off and the pilot started to fly higher and higher, and when we reached seven thousand feet the plane dropped straight down. The captain started sweating and shaking and the pilot shouted at him, "Capi, if you don't want us all to die, take the suitcase with the money, leave us the guns, and I'll lay the plane down softly in La Teresiana. If not, look down, because what's happening is that I'm letting this plane head straight for the dirt. I'm not going to spend one day in jail. Make up your mind." The captain looked at the sergeant, the sergeant looked at the captain, and they gave us the rifles. We landed, we fulfilled our word, and they slipped away: If I see you, I don't know you. They were alone with their ten thousand dollars in the middle of the jungle. First we carried the rock to Brazil and later we jumped over the puddle to land in Guinea Bissau. They called the pilot Palo Seco, Hard Wood, because he didn't do anything if he wasn't drunk. The people gave him that name for fun.

It's said that one time he'd gone to El Chapare in Bolivia to collect a package. He loaded up the merchandise, which was headed to Cali, but two helicopters showed up at the head of the runway. The man advised them by radio that if they didn't knock off the shit they were pulling he'd knock them over with the plane. He got the plane going full speed, 100 percent, and the helicopters barely had time to get out of the way, but they cleared off. Palo Seco blew past them in a hail of gunfire and managed to land the plane at Leticia with more holes in it than a Nazarene. We Colombians leave our mark.

Just like Frijolito, a Caquetá guy from El Doncello, who declared war on the Leopards and the DEA.[2] He turned up dead and they never said that he'd taken two Leopards and a DEA agent with him. They said that they'd taken him alive and then tore him to pieces. They do it because they know that nobody reclaims the body of a Colombian found dead in Peru or Bolivia. Next to the police from those countries, the Colombians are little nuns from the Salvation Army.

Out of Peru, and from the Huayagas region alone, we Colombians transported five or six hundred thousand kilos of damp paste and, later, when the hicks learned how to do it, many other kilos of low-grade cocaine sulphate. Now they are shipping many tons of crystal. Nevertheless, everything that moves out is overseen by Colombians. The Peruvians and the Bolivians have tried to get involved in Colombia, but they haven't been able. We don't let them. How many Bolivians work in Colombian laboratories? Zero, not one. How many Colombians work in Peru or Bolivia? Here alone, in the Cochabamba jail, there are twenty five guys from my country. Every one of them in for drug trafficking, except for one jerk who killed his wife. Of course you have to look closely at who's filling their pockets from this business. For a kilo of crystal we Colombians pocket let's say ten thousand dollars, and the monkeys sell it for twenty five thousand. What happens to the fifteen thousand pieces of green in between? Perhaps it's the Americans, each coming in turn for their hit? This network of distribution is the most complicated, which added to ours moves more than two hundred tons of 90 percent pure crystal every year. That's without taking into account horse, which is selling like hotcakes. In a little while no one's going to be talking about Colombian parakeet but rather Colombian horse, which on its own isn't the highest grade stuff. But almost.

The network spends much less than it has in reserve to cover its bets, to stay clear of eradication, seizures, and wars. It's like saying the water that runs through the pipes in the city is the same water that's in the reservoirs. It's not saying the pipes are storage. In the drug market it's the same. In the networks and the little streams people stockpile for the time when things get tight. That's why prices stay more or less the same despite the hard shots they give us, despite the eradication and the stunts they try. Furthermore, you have to realize that the middleman whose merchandise has been seized lowers his prices in order to get back on his feet. The growers do the same: they plant more in direct relation to how often the other side sprays. That's why I say that every time there's more cocaine, every time it's cheaper and it's purer. We keep the gringo market supplied in full.

During one of those scarce times I made a connection to buy five thousand kilos of crystal along the banks of Lake Chamí. Cocaine grown in El Chapare, of very high quality and selling at a good price. I set up in business with a Bolivian and made a deal with a man I knew who flew a luxury commander; an ex-official of the Colombian air force who knew all the airports on the Santa Cruz–Cali–Gulf of Mexico line. What's more, he knew how many military and civilian personnel worked for the DEA, because he collaborated with the Americans on many occasions. They called him Tinkertoy. We carried the merchandise in several suitcases, and our job was to move it as far as La Guajira in order to ship it on a Galician airbus directly to Europe. We had the line well oiled and humming, 95 percent spoken for. The other 5 percent was managed by Carchi, my Bolivian coworker.

The day we were leaving Santa Cruz for the point of departure, I woke up on the wrong side of the bed. I said to Tinkertoy, "Brother, this job stinks like a stiff to me. Something's out of place with the plan. I'm going to leave the pistol behind so I'm not carrying anything that will betray me." When it was a dangerous job, I was always in the habit of carrying the R-15 with me. But since I had the hunch that we had been betrayed, I decided that, no, I would leave it behind. Nevertheless, at the moment we were going out, Carchi handed me a Baretta and said, "It's better to bring it."

We flew over the spot. Everything was in order, but just the same I was still uneasy, and I said to Tinkertoy, "Brother, you're not going to land. Let's go back because I can't shake this uneasiness." Carchi blew his top and treated me like a coward. I said, "OK, we'll leave it to God." We landed. Carchi got out first and walked toward a two-lane road at the side of the landing strip. Just as he was getting there, a man wearing green goggles walked out, saluted, and then embraced him. Right then I realized we were surrounded. Leopards rushed out on all sides, heavily camouflaged and with their guns raised. I threw the Baretta off to the side so they wouldn't grab me with my hand in the cookie jar, because around here that crime is good for twenty-five years if you're lucky.

They handcuffed us and loaded us up tied hands and feet, like goats, in the pen of a military vehicle. Six hours of bouncing around until we arrived at a barracks that they shared with the DEA in the jungle of El Chapare, called Santa Lucía. A training center for the special antidrug forces, with an airport that accommodates planes like the Galaxies, which can hold five helicopters in their belly.

They took us out of the car with our heads covered and, while smacking us around, brought us to a room that must have been a big hall, because there was an echo. First the interrogation with our faces covered. You lose contact with the interrogator's voice and you don't know where the blows are coming from. Carchi said to me, "I'm going to talk." I told him, "Not me." He pleaded with me to confess, and I answered, "Colombians don't give people up, not even informers. You're a traitorous son of a bitch." Then they gave me the little hat: they pushed my head into a pool of water until I nearly drowned, and, when I had already turned purple, they let me breathe. This didn't work for them either. Then they covered my face with a caustic spray that nearly drove me mad. As if I had fallen into acid or had raw garlic rubbed in my eyes. Nothing came of this either. Your connections not only keep you alive but, at the moment of truth, they're your livelihood. They really gave me a beating, hitting me with balls and giving me raps on the ears. Finally a forensic specialist came and examined me. A shyster who'd sign anything. They did the same to Tinkertoy and, after they threw me in a corner, I heard everything. The guy cried but he didn't talk either. He also must have known that the only beneficiary if we talked was Carchi, the one who betrayed us and got fat on the payoff.

I never killed in anger, because it was always my job to do it in someone else's name. With Carchi it would have been different; I would have killed him with pleasure, and I'm sure I would forgive myself.

Hanged Man

Those of us born and raised in Armero lost track of our memories. That night was the first night I was on my own, with nothing left. We slept in the mud; my parents were buried forever, so were my brothers, my friends, the streets of the town where I learned how to play, the church where I took my first communion on June 21, the house where I was born, a great house with wings and three courtyards: the garden patio, the patio with trees, and the one for the horses where my uncle's horse arrived one morning with him riding on it dead, hoisted upon the cross, his feet and face the color of mulberry and his body stretched out to its full length like a fish on a plate. My father untied him without shedding a single tear and then laid him half down on the ground, because my uncle was already stiff from being dead. Desquite had killed him at the Las Animas School, above La Victoria. Without knowing that he did it, Desquite had set the trap for my uncle's death in front of some municipal buildings built by the Conservatives, and my uncle died because, even though he wasn't a conservative, he arrived just when the liberals were killing them, one by one. First they threw them out of the dumptruck in which they arrived, then they dragged them into a classroom, and finally they snapped their necks in the ditch with a wooden stake. My uncle they put back on his horse instead of leaving him on the pile of dead bodies; it was their way of asking forgiveness for their mistake. My father must have taken it that way, because he never talked about the incident after we buried my uncle in that same garden courtyard; the cemetery was forbidden to liberals after April 9, the day they killed Armero's priest, who had fired on Gaitán's followers from the church tower, they being the ones who demanded the head of the mayor as a payback for the head of their leader. All this was buried beneath the earth when the landslide started that night and didn't stop cascading down, burying every detail of the town.

I wasn't living there because I had gone in those days to study auto mechanics at the Sena in Ibagué. My dream was to learn combine mechanics, those machines as big as factories that harvest rice and wheat, thresh the grain, and, then to top it all off, pack it into sacks. From when I was a kid these machines astonished me, and since we didn't own land, it fell to us to work on what others owned. That morning, when I was cleaning up before heading out to class, my roommate said to me, "Don Yamit's gone crazy. Listen to what he's saying: Armero disappeared. Does that mean they'll have to change the celebration of Holy Innocents' Day?" But from the moment I heard the radio announcer giving the news, I knew it was true. When I went out to the street to look toward the town, all the neighbors were talking about the same thing, as if all of us were carrying candles in the same funeral procession. Everyone was in the street talking and making predictions at the same time, but no one believed that it was possible that a large town like Armero, a town with a mayor, an honorable city council, health department, park, taxis, airport, team of firemen, bank, and old folks home, could disappear overnight. No one believed that the mountain could spew out so much mud, and, above all, no one could explain why. But that's how it was.

I did the same as my father did with my uncle. I cried as far as the cemetery, or, to be honest, until the large Mass for the dead in Guay-abal, and then I returned to my machines. I dropped mechanics and specialized in electricity, which is what makes cars move. The electric cylinder always seemed to me the rarest and strangest thing of all. This instrument, generating electricity simply by revolving, was for me a miracle, and it still is.

The electric cylinder helped keep a lid on my pain, although Ade-laida—a woman from Ibagué with light blue eyes and long, shapely legs who studied at the Young Women's School—helped me too. I started to fall in love with her, inviting her for ice cream in Murillo Toro Park and a stroll along the avenues instead of going to class. We walked along looking in the store windows. I didn't say much because

I was afraid, and she laughed at my timidity. I kept on loving her until one day I proposed to her. She didn't understand what I was saying, and she told me I was crazy because we weren't even dating. So I told her that I would tie everything up in one package, making one declaration in place of two. She had other boyfriends, and, in order to get rid of them, I made up my mind to ask her to marry me; if she said no, I would leave her on her own, and, if she said yes, she would have to drop her boyfriends. We were married in the church right away. We spent our honeymoon dancing to salsa at the fair in Cali. She was a good listener and she danced well. She wanted a lot of things, but since I was in love I couldn't see where we were headed.

From Sena I went out to work in a repair shop, and from there I took a job with the Paláez Brothers, recharging batteries. Don Augusto Pinillos, the boss, took an interest in me and helped me to get a job in the auto shop. Since I knew all about electricity and had a knack for figuring it out, they made me head of the department. I was there three years, working with cables, alternators, spark plugs, until I was no longer a mystery but a nuisance to my wife. Elias, the first of our sons, was born and we were still going to the fairs in Cali to kick off the year dancing to salsa. I liked dancing with her because when you dance you're happy and oblivious. Adelaida liked to dress well and show off a new outfit each day of the fair. At times she let me know the things she didn't have and gave me the business about it. I was in love, so I gave her everything she wanted, even if there was no bread in the house or milk for the baby.

Around that time I got a job in Medellín. Since I knew so much about electricity and had the technical side down, my bosses paid for a course in injection carburetors given by the Crump Company. I scored the highest in the class, and they offered to make me head of a repair shop specializing in keeping race cars in shape, with a better salary and better conditions. I talked about it with Adelaida and we made the move to Bella Villa. Although the business operated under the name Velez Autos, the truth, which I would discover later, was that the owner was Roberto Gaviria. A good man, I can't deny it, generous toward those who worked hard for him and straight up with those who treated him straight. He was Don Pablo's friend, whom I had the honor of knowing back in those days.[1] Together they were a good pair, and, since they weren't short of cash, they kept their cars in top condition with the latest of the latest. They were in love with the adventure of speed. Life and death always walk together, but on a racetrack the play between them is easier to see. They dance around unseen in front of the driver.

These two—I'm talking about Pablo and Roberto—were true friends, almost one person. Sometimes they were so attuned it was scary, because what one had gone through the other had too, even when they weren't together. On the racetrack you could see how well they fit together. From cars to women, they'd been inseparable since they were kids. They were together in Argentina when Don Severo went to live in Buenos Aires, invited by Peron to work as a laborer. They carried themselves like important little men when they went together to Boca Junior.[2] Doña Hermilda, Pablo's mother, had a small dress shop and her handiwork was so fine that Evita herself gave her business making her clothes. They say that Evita was Colombian and maybe that's why she came to love the lady, her husband, and the kids so much. Pablo and Roberto talked about her as if she were still alive.

They worked together in Medellín, dealing parts on bicycles, and that's where their love of speed and danger was born. They brought the markets to the boulevards of El Poblado and flew down those hills as fast as their bicycles would carry them. They wanted to race in the Tour de Colombia, and that's where Roberto Escobar, the Little Bear—how he flew!—carried off the prize for bikes. Later, still together, they dedicated themselves to robbing bronze from the gravestones in the local cemeteries and then selling them all over Antioquia. Let's say they would arrive in Jardin and find out who was about to die; with the bronze that they picked up at night from the monuments, they made new ornaments with the names of those about to pass away, so that when they did die, they already had engravings with the dead person's dates on it. They made enough money to buy a car, until they discovered that it was cheaper, instead of so much drudgery, searching and traveling, to steal cars and buy the papers for them. They were decent guys; what they had lost was their discovery that it wasn't worth it to work, that the authorities were cronies up to their necks in corruption.

I kept their cars in shape for them from top to bottom. They competed all over with the cars and had the funds to buy and convert them into the best in the country. They paid for me to take a class in English over the course of six months, so that I could go on my own to the U.S. and Europe to bring them the latest parts that appeared on the market. On one of the trips Adelaida, already mother of our second son, Lisandro, came along with me. She was still pretty and the air in New York went to her head. She liked everything she saw, taking a sudden fancy to what she wasn't able to afford and coveting what belonged to others. It made me feel bad because she was going about comparing me with my bosses, until she ended up treating me like a coward. Finally, I smacked her in plain sight in Central Park, and from that day things began to go sour. That night we went out to dance real salsa at a bar in Queens, and she became infatuated with a black guy from the Dominican Republic, which made me realize that Cali, the one with the fairs, was now long gone.

I arrived back in Colombia poisoned, as if my camshaft was getting out of whack. I brought Don Roberto an electric injector, one of the first in the country, and bought another for myself, or, to tell the truth, to sell to the competition, a bad idea since the Escobars had a lot of confidence in me. I made a few bucks at the price of disloyalty, but I justified myself by going along with the game that Adelaida was playing on me.

The next trip I made was to Europe, to the World Auto Show in Turin, where the fastest cars and the latest innovations were on display. Don Roberto traveled with me and he carried himself like a king. I made a few side trips on my own too and managed to bring back auto parts unknown in Colombia. I sold them secretly to Don Joselin Prieto, our most dangerous rival, a man whose driving ambition was to be in charge. In the test runs he would keep in mind the movements of every machine, with a fine ear for each one. He didn't make mistakes, he didn't boast, and he was as accurate as a piston. That's why he knew how to win. The Escobars envied and, what's more, hated him, although he never did anything to them. He suggested that I come to work in his shop, but I liked being a double agent more, as it was dangerous. The Escobars were tough customers and they didn't go for betrayal, no matter how small. Nevertheless, I kept at it so I could get my hands on the things I wanted.

In one of the last trips that I made for them I met a guy from Cúcuta on the plane, an agent for Pegasus Airlines. We became friends talking about the role that gear size plays in a vehicle's power and speed, whether it's a truck, a car, or a tractor. He knew a lot and we ended up sharing a few shots. His name was Galo Domínguez. In Madrid I invited him to the hotel where I was staying and between one thing and another told him about my life. My whole life. He knew how to drag the secrets out of me, from my relationship with the Escobars even so far as life with Adelaida, which in those days was going from bad to worse. He was flattering me up to the point that he proposed we go into business together on spare parts. I listened to him closely and he hustled me along until we closed the deal and formed a business. We bought parts secondhand in Spain and sold them in Colombia as if they were new. There was a big difference in price, and business was good. He offered to process the import papers, because in those days the system of preliminary permits was still in effect. He bought the material in Madrid and I took it to Colombia. There were no clouds anywhere on the horizon. Adelaida traveled much of the time and we ended up buying an apartment in Madrid.

The business really began to take off, going from a few little dollars to several thousand in less than six months. The man was watching me, but I was doing the same as he was, making Adelaida happy, since now she had a good apartment, a late model car, and the dresses she craved. We spent our vacations in Cartagena and Aruba. We were almost rich and she went with me wherever I went. Even so, I knew I couldn't ease up, because then the whole operation would fall apart.

One day Galo laid out for me what he was studying carefully: "Let's start an export line, sending tombs to Europe." "Tombs?" "That's right, tombs! We'll buy fake Indian tombs, take care of the business part quickly, and send them off to Europe by certified mail or as unaccompanied luggage. We'll pick them up at Atocha Station, break the seals, take out the product—the nut—sell it, use the money to buy spare parts, and ship them to Colombia by regular mail. A straightforward business, a winner in every respect."

I doubted it. Right then and there I pointed out every kind of difficulty until—I have to say it even though it hurts—I gave in for fear that Adelaida would go back to treating me like a coward. I ended up agreeing and spent many sleepless nights until I had perfected the plan. Later we passed from words to deeds: Looking for a craftsman for the tombs, finding the coke in Pereira, investigating certified mail. We spent seventeen months greasing the wheels. During the year we made five full shipments of spare parts, all of them legal and clean, until we'd arranged a solid base to begin working for real.

We talked about whether the first shipment ought to be a test run or the real thing. Galo and Adelaida convinced me to start out with a pair of clay jugs with thick sides to see if the merchandise could be shipped without any trouble. The tombs arrived in perfect condition, with each one carrying five kilos. The idea couldn't have been more brilliant: X rays didn't detect anything and, since these were objects of great artistic value, customs wasn't able to break them open.

I went ahead by myself, with nothing on me. While the package was arriving I made it my job to buy everything we needed in spare parts to send to Colombia because the exportation of tombs was going on for real. Our plan wasn't to use up all our time on this job but to limit ourselves to big shipments and work legally on the spare parts we'd purchased. Buy some land, an apartment, and take it easy the rest of the way.

When Galo phoned me to say that everything was ready, I thought about getting out of the affair. But it wasn't easy by then. I hung up the phone and sent a big shipment of spare parts to Colombia. Fifty thousand dollars worth. While they were traveling on the water, the tombs were flying through the air. I was all set up at the Phoenix Hotel in Centro Colón, just like I was a rich guy, with all my papers in order, a car and driver. I waited and waited. Everyday I had long phone conversations with Adelaida; we talked about a little of everything in order to keep my mind off the subject. Sometimes I headed down to the lobby in order to make a show of the fact that I was a very wealthy and important businessman. I got up late, dressed slowly, ate breakfast at eleven, had lunch at four, made a spin through the park at the Prado, and then went from bar to bar, discotheque to discotheque, sex shop to sex shop, looking at all the porn films showing in Madrid at that time.

Then one morning I got news that the package had arrived. I dressed to the nines, said a prayer for myself, and went up to the claims window. I made a full circuit around the post office trying to find out if it was a set up. Everything seemed normal to me. I arrived at the claims window and the lady employee asked me to go through the door, because the package wouldn't fit through the opening in the window. I went in, they asked me to wait a minute, and after a few moments they led me into another room, where I saw the famous package just as Galo had described it to me. They asked me if I was so-and-so. "Yes, that's me." "You came to claim this package?" "Yes." "The number is a match for the receipt you brought. OK, please sign the receipt with your full name." I had just finished signing when the man who had asked the questions identified himself: Guardia Civil, Elite Antidrug Taskforce, District Attorney's Office. I stood stock still, thunderstruck. I thought about throwing myself out the window. But no: the four men surrounded me.

I immediately realized that I had fallen in a trap, a trap set with patience, step by step, by Galo. He had used me like a blind piece of bait, and at that very hour he was already receiving the spare parts. The whole shipment, clean down to the smallest detail. He had tricked me as he would a kid.

One of the cops broke into the sarcophagus with the butt of his pistol. Inside was a small thin package, wrapped in plastic. They opened it, weighed it, and a forensic specialist gave the verdict: two kilos, three hundred and twenty grams, 95 percent pure. One of the guards handed me a small piece of paper from inside the package, which read, "Love and Kisses. Yours, Adelaida."

I shouted at the cops that they were on the take, I had nothing to do with the package, I was the victim of a trick, I wasn't waiting for a container but an artifact, I was an exporter of spare parts, an electrical mechanic by profession, I made my living at it, I did so honorably, I knew nothing about anything. "Nothing about anything," the cops repeated while they put handcuffs on me and threw me in a car that went to the Plaza de Castilla. When we arrived everything of mine from the hotel was already there, including a suitcase with 280,000 pesetas that I had left over from my purchases and had set aside for myself. They asked me my date of birth, made me sign papers, gave me a staff lawyer, and pushed me toward the showers. I jumped back, pleading that I didn't shower in cold water because I had bad kidneys. "Kidneys?" said one of the guards, and he shoved me so hard I fell on the floor. I opened the shower door and bathed with my clothes on. They forced me to strip and gave me a thorough rubdown with lice soap.

I came out covered with sweat and shaking from the cold. I cried like a young girl who had just lost her virginity. I didn't argue. I surrendered to my fate and let myself go where the river wanted to carry me. The hours passed. My head was a mishmash where Galo and Adelaida appeared, a gold statue and the hotel room, the Guardia Civil and the import license, Don Roberto and my uncle. They spun around, playing in my head: Adelaida dancing, Adelaida kissing me, Adelaida buying dresses, Adelaida and her light blue eyes and long shapely legs. I fell asleep without knowing it. The cold woke me up many times until dawn came and I opened my eyes. I thought everything was a movie. I couldn't believe where I was now, when only hours before I was making plans to return to Colombia. A couple of hard punches snapped me out of my daydreams, shots that struck me like a stone through the grates of the cell. Good God! Where am I ? Am I going crazy? The guard shouted at me: "You can make a call to Colombia if you want."

I called Adelaida. A maid answered. She told me that two days before she had taken the kids to sleep at her sister's, that she hadn't returned, and that she had given orders that if I called she wished me good luck and a steady hand to get out of where I had fallen. That she prayed to the Virgin for me. I fell down when it hit me. The only guilty party was myself, for not making up my mind to get rid of her. I went over to the basin and washed my face. I took my dentures out of my mouth and placed them on the edge of the sink. I wanted to get really dirty, I dropped my pants and shat out everything I had. As I was buttoning up my pants I knocked my dentures by mistake, and they fell into a hole in the bathroom floor. A deep hole. I reached into it but there wasn't any bottom. I started shouting desperately and crying. I felt around inside my toothless mouth, panicked and decided to kill myself. I tied one end of my belt around my neck and the other to a water pipe that hung from the ceiling. I let go. The pressure made me feel like my eyes were going to explode.

I woke up in the infirmary. Two psychologists tried to calm me down and a nurse gave me pills while another rubbed alcohol on my throat, because the tightening of the belt had left a long black and blue mark on my neck. A few days later they sent me to Carabanchel to live with my memories in a cell from which neither I nor my memories can escape.

What I really need is an avalanche like the one in Armero, so I'd be buried alive.

Eight Years, Three Months, One Day

Even after the High Court of Appeals ruled against me they couldn't convince me of my guilt. I always felt that the magistrates had the wrong person, that they were talking about someone else, and that the person in jail was living in a dream. But from the day the lawyer read me the sentence I began to doubt myself until I concluded that the one who was wrong was me. I lived eight years of my life from minute to minute—start to finish—and I survived owing to my three daughters, who finished growing up without me, while I, in the prison at Carabanchel, began to grow old.

They weren't daughters of the same father. The oldest I had with Oscar, a young kid I met in college and who, when my brother died, became my refuge. I went about dying from his death. He was older, always pale and always absent; he lived as if he were in the other life even before he died. One day he stopped going to college, then he stopped eating, and finally he stood in the window incessantly looking into the distance, as if he was waiting for someone. My mother told me that I was to blame and that's why I married poor Oscar, who never knew why I had chosen him as my husband.

We separated on the night that, lying side by side in bed, he got the idea to ask about my brother. I answered every one of his suspicions one after the other. But he kept coming back to it, digging in deeper and always wanting more truth, and even more, until I got up and went down to the street to sleep. He followed me there with his persecution, until I told him that if he kept asking I would tell him what nobody wants to hear. So he hit me. I hit him too, and we ended up tearing each other's eyes out. The next day I gathered up my things and went back to my house. I returned to college too, to finish up my degree because maybe I wanted to be somebody. I graduated and went with the flow.

I had my eye on Nicanor since I was a kid. I watched him get married, have four sons with a woman he detested, leave her, and then come to my house to ask for my hand in marriage. My mother said that she would speak with me, and I told him that I would be his wife but not his mother, that the two of us could live together but I wasn't going to love him or look out for him. He accepted, and at the end of a year, when we were getting ready for a trip to El Cerrejon, the first of the girls we had together was born. He is a topographer; he measures distances. He worked on measuring the world's largest open-air carbon mine, but when he finished he was out of work. During that time my last daughter was born, and we were what we were: nine people of flesh and blood, each one of whom you had to take care of and watch over according to his good or bad disposition. It would be easier to take all the carbon out of the mine with one shovel.

He was unemployed, I was unemployed, we were all unemployed. We weren't even able to get a house, which is the one thing you need in order to be unemployed in peace. We all squeezed into my mother's house, which had always been the in-between spot for me, but with the husband and seven children it turned into hell. That's the way it was from the moment I put the smallest one down in the living room so I could change her diapers. That's why, when Nicanor's sister Juliana called me on the phone from Madrid, and she invited me to "a housekeeping job wherever you look," I didn't doubt the future for all of us was Spain. She had gone there several years before; she ran a cafeteria and she had managed to make a life for herself. She assured me that she would help me find work and school for the boys—who were his— and for the girls—who were mine.

Nicanor had an inheritance left him by his father, a small piece of land over in Garagoa and a house in town. He sold them both, and with that we had enough to buy plane tickets for Madrid and we left on the first of the month. The month went by quickly and we hadn't managed to get an apartment so we could live on our own. I got a job as a service employee. (What they call an attendant here goes by the name *day-time help* in Colombia.) But my husband wanted to work in his field, topography, and he wouldn't agree to look for a job that

Eight Years, Three Months, One Day

made him feel in a lesser position. Exactly at that time they passed a law that required Colombians to obtain a work permit, for which we had to have, first of all, a residence, and only wealthy Colombians who had friends with pull in the government could fulfill that condition. Or to put it differently, it fell to us to look really hard for any place we could find, because we didn't even have food, a place to sleep, or any way to get back home.

Nicanor was on the brink. Arrogant and timid, he went out to see what jobs were available, what kind of work they could offer him, without looking at how we were doing and what our daily reality was. I took two jobs as an assistant. One from eight in the morning until two in the afternoon and the other from three in the afternoon to nine at night. I came back to the house only to sleep, because I had no desire to eat the food they gave me. The next day I pestered him again not to let us become homeless.

I worked the first shift in the house of rich Colombians and the second in the apartment of a Lebanese couple, both men, very strange people in their tastes and routines. They were night birds. I woke them up when I arrived, when it was already three in the afternoon, and I never knew what they did. They slept apart, each one in his bed, but they kissed each other as if they were very much in love.

The Colombian family was even more difficult. They almost never went out of the house, no one ever visited them, they had no children. She read magazines and he watched television until one, at which time he poured himself a brandy, called for lunch, and kept on drinking brandy until he began to sing "Yesterday's Waves."[1] He lay on the sofa sleeping, and when he woke up he went to bed with his wife. They didn't say much to each other. Even so, from time to time they took off together, they were gone three or four days and they came back happy, as if they had pulled off some kind of mischief.

One day they told me to clean up the mess on the first floor because a Colombian was coming to work for them as a gardener. It struck me as strange but I cleaned up, swept the place, and put things away. The gardener arrived, left his suitcase in his room, and went off to get drunk with his boss. Strange. Nonetheless, fine, acceptable, the compatriot coming from where he was coming. The next day the same and the next after that. And the garden? Nothing. What garden? They spent all day drinking, laughing, dancing by themselves. Very strange: a rich Colombian speaking informally with his gardener and even more informally with his wife. No. I couldn't put the puzzle together. There was something fishy. They took off, probably for vacations in Palma de Mallorca, carrying all their suitcases with them, less one. Since they had hired me to keep my eye on the house, I gave myself the job of investigating. Here, there, further inside, further out, until I stumbled on the piece I was looking for: the gardener's suitcase, the lining torn on the inside, with traces of a powder that I figured was cocaine. I grabbed my things, closed the house up tight, and told myself, "I'm not coming back, I'm not going to trip up like an imbecile. I didn't come here to be anybody's blind bait. I'm going." And I went.

But you can't live on wishes. We'd been in Spain for a year: Nicanor was stuck in his rut, in spite of my battling him every day, in spite of seeing me about to burst from all my hard work. I couldn't look at him and his kids eating from my labors—already grown-up men who at least should have had the consideration to make their bed, clean their clothes, or take care of their father. Not at all. They didn't pitch in for any of it. I arrived home from work to do their drudgery. My daughters were my daughters, and I lived for them. But those four mastodons weren't even carrying the air that I breathed out.

To settle accounts, the owner of the apartment where we lived started an eviction proceeding, which goes very quickly in Spain. In order to keep the suitcases off the sidewalk with the girls sitting on top of them, I had to ask some other Colombians who were in the same situation but with only two kids for a little bit of room. They shared their apartment while we were getting things together. Scary days. All the kids were fighting between themselves, and Nicanor was flirting with the Colombian woman who lived there: not because he liked her but out of boredom. Lost causes. It didn't matter to me. What a blessing if he had hooked up with her. But what about it? They were both in the same situation, so they couldn't do anything. They spent the whole day bad-mouthing their spouses, us, the ones who actually went out to work.

It was during that time when I jumped into work with a lady from Argentina of whom, little by little, I came to realize that hers was the oldest profession in the world: stealing. She was a thief. Just like it sounds: a thief. She stole, from the lottery tickets in the lobby of a hotel right up to gold necklaces in the jewelry stores. A beautiful woman, not fat but definitely robust, who pulled all the strings. You put up a fight to the death with her once. But the second time you aren't up to it and all the reasons you had marshaled to avoid her become reasons to accept her, to work side by side with her, and even grab hold of her so she can't get away.

One day she said to me, "Look, a good chick like you, making a wiseass, a gigolo, a fool out of your husband. Who does he think he is?" The rolling pin in my stomach dropped. I gave in. She gave me an advance of a third so that I could leave things in order—food for my daughters, the back rent, the dreams still alive—and I took Iberia flight 501, Madrid to Rio to Buenos Aires. I traveled as an Andalusian, a tourist, a widow, a lover of the good life who wanted to enjoy her last quarter of an hour. The truth was the Argentine had to loan me money for the photo I needed to put on the fake passport. It was the last argument in favor of accepting, without delay, what destiny had in store for me.

In Buenos Aires I took a room in a decent hotel. I barely went out of the room for fear that I would be discovered and didn't leave the hotel for fear that the other party would arrive and not find me. One day, two days, three days. I was sick of looking at myself in the mirror, pulling the hairs out of my legs and cutting my nails; I walked around like a busybody, keeping my eye on the people floating around the lobby of the hotel, when I saw a guy arrive whom I only had to see to know that he had arrived for me. There was no doubt. I came to a stop and greeted him as if I knew him. His name was Antonio Goliani. He knew it too: my hunch did not surprise him. On the contrary, he explained to me that he had to wait several days in Mar de Plata because the merchandise had been delayed, but I shouldn't worry. "Everything is going according to plan." He instructed me to keep posing as a tourist, get a tan and play in the casino from time to time, but "you definitely can't fall in love because you're already involved," and, he added, "You understand?" which made a real impression on me.

Time went by. I remember that I came into Tucumán Airport with all the enthusiasm of someone who knows she has but one route. I was keeping an eye on things from as far back on line as possible, so I could avoid pointless and dangerous conversations. When I was in the process of handing over my passport, I suddenly felt the bags taped to the inside of my thigh coming loose. The tension made me sweat, and the sweat was causing the adhesive that held the bags to come undone. My stockings weren't able to hold them up and they began to slip down my leg. Once again I felt like I did in kindergarten when you pee and everybody turns around to see where the smell is coming from. I squeezed my legs shut while they stamped my passport, but then I couldn't walk. The airport, they told me, was full of plainclothes cops. So I shuffled step by step, until someone touched me from behind while I was squeezing the bags together with every ounce of my strength. I spun around, sat down on a sofa, a doctor came over. My "lookout," Antonio, arrived like a guardian angel, hugged and kissed me, and carried me off to his house, saying that I hated airplanes.

Another fifteen days of tanning myself at Mar del Plata and then a change in the flight plan: Caracas, Santo Domingo, Santiago de Campostela, Madrid. This time I crossed the ocean like a tortoise. But when I arrived in Campostela, those of us heading to Madrid had to pass through customs. There was an overhead sign that separated the passengers into Spaniards, Latin Americans, and the rest of the world. I got on line. When I showed my passport, the woman said to me, "Maybe you don't know how to read? Your line is on the other side, lady. What are you doing, thinking that you are going to renounce your nationality? Get moving!" My passport—I had forgotten—was Spanish.

I arrived with the shipment intact. Waiting for me in Madrid was, to my surprise, Antonio. I unloaded, they paid me, and I started to get some feeling back in my legs. I totaled up accounts and took out what we needed for living, month by month, until I figured out that we had enough for the year. Winter clothes included. We took an apartment for ourselves and we were able to go back to the parks with our heads held high. You can't understand how attractive suicide is until you live a winter in Europe sharing an apartment and having to send the kids out to steal from the supermarket.

Life was getting back to normal. Nicanor found a position in an engineering firm that bulldozed land to make way for a highway. My girls were growing and his mastodons were on line one by one for Colombia, which took a load off my shoulders. I kept my job as an attendant, and time returned to its natural rhythm. The future wasn't wide open and winter was threatening to come back again.

Antonio rang me up one day. We met in Plaza Mayor, talked about everything, he asked about my life, my girls, my country, and, when we had already said good-bye, said to me, "No doubt you still have feelings for me," and he kissed me. It affected me deeply. It made me think of when I was fourteen and I dreamt of James Dean. He called me again later to ask me if I could help him find a rental car for a friend who had come from Argentina. I said yes and took it out in my name. A few days later he told me that he knew a Colombian who was interested in doing business with other Colombians. He introduced me to a man in his fifties—Mr. Germán—who he said was the proprietor of a chain of racetracks in the northern part of the Cauca valley and a fruit exporter from the Unión region. Very lordly, he invited us to eat in one of the most luxurious restaurants on Alcalá Street. Without wasting time on details, or, rather, pushing them to the side, he told us that he was in Madrid closing a deal to ship exotic fruits—granadilla, uchuva, and pitahaya—with a Spanish consortium. He shot me complicit looks as he described the fruits, but I didn't make inquiries because the truth is I was already sighing over the Argentine. Over his elegant hands and bony fingers.

Days went by and the Colombian returned for the bullfights in San Isidro. I had never been to see the bulls, and in fact I hated that spectacle of blood and death, but he insisted so much that I ended up going with this Germán, which was the name of the protector given me by the angels. Or the devils. Because that very afternoon I said that yes, I would help to negotiate a container ship full of coconuts that was already docked in the port of La Coruña. I had a friend who worked in the Corte Inglés food store, and I thought—as I said to him—that she, Marcela, could make us number two in the sales department.

In reality, the next day Marcela, after making a thorough inquiry, called me and told me that in the best of cases Corte Inglés could only buy some five thousand coconuts if the price was good for them. Germán didn't object, but he advised me that we wouldn't close up shop unless we couldn't find a place for all the fruit, so that the market wouldn't be overstocked with coconuts and prices fell. That seemed reasonable, although I didn't understand much about money matters. He showed up with an open voucher for the purchase of clothes. "Appearance is everything in this world," he said and he gave me a kiss, calling me his "partner." It annoyed me to hear myself referred to that way, but in the final analysis I didn't want to go back to carrying cocaine from Argentina.

With Corte Inglés business began for real. I had to present my papers in order to nationalize the coconuts, to transport them, to put them on the shelves. Everything was moving ahead with displays of the merchandise and elegant outfits, and, as a Colombian resident in Spain, Germán asked me to store them in my apartment because, as he put it, they couldn't live without the heat that comes from other Colombians. I let him know that it was physically impossible now because there were too many of us in any case to fit into two rooms. He then asked me if I would rent an apartment for him in my name. He thought the business might be put on hold and with the type of visa that he had no one would rent him a piece of real estate. Fine. Little by little I was getting sandwiched in and, what's worse, I did so reluctantly.

Nicanor hired a truck to carry the coconuts from the warehouse in Madrid to all the places—garages, rooms, patios—that we had rented to store them in while the various sales contracts were drawn up. I worked as I had never done before. Something kept me holding back, unhappy, disenchanted with every connection that we made. Germán was making contacts on a higher level. One day he arrived saying that he had lunched with the ambassador, the next with the consul, the next with the secretary of the Department of Commerce, the next with Señor Roldán. It was the first time that I heard this man's name. He showed me photos with this Mr. Roldán. Roldán on the top of the photo, Roldán below.[2] And all of us like little ants, very diligently constructing his defense. Antonio, with whom I drank a glass of wine at the Atocha Station from time to time, where I liked to go so I could feel the heat of the tropics in the hall full of banana trees, morichal and quiché palms, calmed me down by saying that Germán was more of a parvenu than an evildoer. In any case, I quit my domestic jobs and committed myself completely to carrying the coconuts around.

One night Nicanor arrived in a new car that Germán had bought in order to make the job easier for us. This struck me as stranger than everything else, but I let it pass, along with so many other things that made me uncomfortable and even kept me awake from time to time. Nevertheless, life carries you to the rendezvous and neither doubts nor clarity will prevail. We went straight to the spot where we had to arrive.

One day I left the apartment like I did every day, at eight, in order to leave my youngest daughter, who was three years old at the time, at the nursery. I stopped in order to meet Nicanor for a meal at three in the afternoon and would go later to pick up a license at the Department of Industry. I had to get my daughter before six, but Nicanor didn't arrive, and when I walked out of the restaurant, a plainclothes cop came up to me and said, "Come with me." "Go with you?" I asked, surprised and upset. "Where?" "Lady," he answered me, "Just a few questions at the police station and then you'll be free." "But what is it about?" I demanded. "It's just routine," he answered, and then I heard a police car pull up with its siren on. They shoved me in and took me to the precinct. The commissioner asked me if they had read me my rights, and right after they lead me to the narcotics office. I started screaming like a madwoman: "This can't be, it can't be, something's wrong; my daughter, my daughter, let me go get her at six before they put her in the street and a car kills her, for the love of God, officers. It's an outrage; I want my lawyer, my husband. Call the ambassador." The narcotics officer—the narc—asked me to calm down, and he gave me permission to make a telephone call. I called Antonio so that he would pick up my daughters. It was the only important thing at that moment.

A bit calmer, the narc said to me, "Look, lady, your case isn't going to be resolved anytime soon, but if you start to work with us we can help you out. You have the right to an attorney and, if you don't want one, we will assign one to you." He gave me list of proper names and aliases, with photos, so I would tell him who I knew. "You don't have to deny it because you have told us that you are innocent. We believe you and step by step we are going to prove it." The truth was that I didn't know anyone, except Antonio, and Antonio was something else. I couldn't betray him, but what if they really had proofs of my friendship with him? What if he was being held? My doubts began turning into very real bars on my jail cell.

I just said *no* to everything. They took me, at something like nine at night, to an open courtyard. Seated in a corner, frazzled, was Nicanor and, on the other side, Marcela, my friend from the Corte Inglés. From Nicanor's pickup they began unloading, counting, and numbering those blessed coconuts. They made a pile in the middle of the courtyard. The narc called for someone to bring him a hammer and right in front of us he started smashing coconut after coconut. Some of them burst apart, their milk flying all over the officer, others broke and the smuggled goods fell out; in this case, 90 percent pure crystal, white as mother of pearl. Four hours they were there splitting coconuts. Some yes, others no. Some with a prize, others not. In the end: twenty-six kilograms of cocaine, weighed on a scale certified by the judge. I couldn't stand up and couldn't even look at what came out of the coconuts, because my entire body was convulsed in tears. When I signed I no longer knew who I was, what I had signed, or where I was.

Eight Years, Three Months, One Day

Not knowing where the other twenty six thousand coconuts were tortured me for awhile, for if they had been filled by the same hand they would have held the equivalent of more than two tons of cocaine. It distressed me to think that from one moment to the next they could turn up and fatten the charges against us. I was held incommunicado for three days, interrogated in my two-square-meter cell. They didn't mistreat me physically, but my daughters' fate turned into torture. Smoking cigarettes with a filter was prohibited, maybe because with burned plastic you could make the knives with which more than one person had committed suicide. Suicide is an idea that makes the rounds when you convince yourself that the woman behind bars is the real one, the one there forever.

In the wagon in which they transported us from jail I met Nicanor and Marcela once again. He was headed to Carabanchel, the two of us to Yeserias. He told me that he had learned that the girls were well cared for, that Germán had disappeared, and that no matter what happened we were innocent. I felt how brave and tender he was toward me. Prison did that which freedom denied us.

When we arrived at Yeserias, a large prison two blocks long, with two floors and two wings, the prisoners were on strike because the warden had restricted the authorizations for and the length of phone communications. The prisoners made a hellish racket hitting their aluminum plates against the bars. They put us in two security cells while the doctors, the psychologists, and the sociologists examined us and the guards got acquainted. Before passing through the ordinary cellblocks they supplied us with blankets, sheets, towels, uniforms— these were optional—and bathroom supplies. I arrived at my cell dragging my duffel bag as if it were my soul itself. I almost didn't make it. The girls continued to torment me day and night. The Municipality of Madrid had taken charge of them and placed them in an orphanage for the daughters of drug-addicted mothers and fathers. The girls knew how to live poor but not alone, because they were never lacking for love; I was always anxious for them and always at their side making sure that the world did them the least possible damage. But life is very jealous and won't let anyone take control of it. Looking to protect them, I ended up leaving them abandoned. But they knew how to move ahead on their own, as they promised me in their first letter. "Mamí, don't worry about us. In spite of all the jails you will still be our mamá and the strength that you gave us won't let us cower under the bed crying. If you are well, so are we." But I cried thinking about them as alone as I was in this cold cell, in the hands of arbitrary power. I also wept for my sadness. A long and dry sobbing without anyone to sympathize. The oldest one spent three days in the infirmary because she fought with another child who had insulted her by calling her "southern narco nigger." For me it was very hard, but my daughter's swagger made me proud. "Mamí," she wrote me, "What is it about us Colombians that they hate so much? Where do we get so much strength to defend ourselves?"

The judge found me guilty of the crimes of drug trafficking and concealment. The prosecuting attorney asked for fourteen years, eight months, and twenty five days, and the judge took down the charges and the punishment as if he weren't a judge but a secretary. They proved that the apartment where the coconuts were found was in my name, that the car that transported them was too, that the steps taken to find other outlets for the coconuts were as well, and that my husband had transported the merchandise. The one thing they couldn't prove was that I knew. My brief regarding the contacts I made to sell the fruit to Corte Inglés didn't matter at all, neither did saying that it was Germán who had delivered the coconuts to us, because he wasn't anywhere to be found; the apartment was in my name and I had no more details about the man than that he liked coconuts. Where were they, furthermore, the twenty six thousand missing coconuts? By the time I was about to get out I knew that one such Germán had his throat slit in Envigado[3] and, when they uncovered the Roldán case, the man appeared in one photograph hugging him. Every defense that I tried to interpose sunk me deeper, until I resolved to keep quiet and accept the lesser guilty charges. I appealed to the superior court, which lowered the punishment to eight years, three months, and a day. It's the jail term we call National Identity because they give it to all of us Colombians.

Prison is hard from start to finish. There is nevertheless a dark, repetitive stretch from which few memories remain and that exists in between the two points of the sentence.

I stayed in Yeserias, which for a long time was a woman's prison, for almost a year. I had serious trouble with a woman from Extremadura. She was tall, wore trainman's boots, pants, a jacket, and a tie. She was a butch who had to be feared and had to have respect. She was in the habit of being called Mr. Carlos. One day she was going down the main stairs and I was coming up because the warden had called for me, and when she passed me she shoved me with her shoulder and bitched at me that I hadn't said hello. On another occasion I ran into her again, and she said to me, "Don't wander around from here to there like a gypsy. When I want a girl like you, little one, it's because you look good to me." And she grabbed my face with her hands loaded with rings and brought me close to her mouth. Furious, I tore her hands off me and she grabbed me by the hair. I managed to get hold of her by the belt and sit her down, until I drove her half crazy with several blows to the back of her head. It was hard for me coming in to be able to stay among those women. The prison directors saw nothing, because in jail silence is the law.

I worked in the tailor shop. We sewed the uniforms for the prisoners, for nurses and soldiers. The routine was a way to suspend time, to make it pass, to reduce authority to a single functionary. We left our cells at breakfast and after breakfast we went to work; later there was the midday meal, then work, the shower, and at last to bed. For everyone of these stages of the day there is a foreman, or, more accurately, a forewoman. She is the one who serves you the best piece of chicken, who hands out the least strenuous work, who lets you wash up in peace. These forewomen belong to organizations and the organizations have unions that have leaders. The directors of the prison negotiate with them, they back them up in order to screw someone, to humiliate them and bring them down. It just so happens that in Spain prisoners have rights: you can complain to your family members and they can raise a ruckus with San Quintin.[4] Getting around those rights are the powers inside the jail, whose rule cannot be appealed.

You are either with them or against them. The worst thing, which strikes me as the most corrupt, is that these guards are used against the inmates, because the prison bosses manipulate them in exchange for favors from the syndicate heads.

One day they called me and ordered me to pack my bag. I was very afraid because I thought they were going to send me to the prison in Alicante, which has a reputation for being tough. But no, they sent me to Carabanchel.

Carabanchel is a very large prison—a small city—with one area for men and another for women. High walls, cold and sad. In the winter they make you want to howl and in the summer they make you feel that the men are close by, maybe there, just over the walls; it's more pain. In Carabanchel half the prisoners are there for drug trafficking and half of those are Colombians. In the office of the cellblock they gave me blankets, sheets, towels, bathroom items, a uniform for the summer and one for the winter. They assigned me to the C-3 dormitory; the guard for that section brought me over and he pointed out from a distance the place where I was to live for many days to come. Every single one of the inmates' faces filled me with overwhelming fear; to me they were women capable of doing anything whose crimes weren't in the past but in the future.

I entered the cellblock taking one step after another, feeling their eyes all over me, some of them caressing, some asking questions, some hating me.

They weren't even done settling me in my cell when a Chilena, Noelia, came up to me and asked, very softly, if I could let her boyfriend have my bunk. I didn't understand. I didn't know anything about mixed cells. She saw my confusion, understood, and explained to me that her boyfriend was a woman too, and that they had waited a long time for the change so that they could be together. "It's no problem for me," I told her, and I sat myself down in the bunk that Noelia left. But the boyfriend gave German classes in the town of Carabanchel and came back late. I don't know if Noelia didn't tell her or if she'd fallen asleep waiting for her: what happened was that the boyfriend jumped in my bunk—where she always slept—thinking I was Noelia. I heard her arrive and lie down, but I was paralyzed with fear. I let her show me how tender she could be, even though she didn't know who I was. She gave up, but there wasn't a scandal. Noelia didn't make one either. You need so much tenderness in prison, so much that you even accept a sincere caress.

They sent a dirty, conniving black woman from Nigeria to the cell-block. She ate with her hands and had a court of black women at her service, all of them in for drug trafficking and, according to them, in charge of the hashish trade. From the time I came in, the black woman gave me the evil eye. She wanted to discipline me, to make me work for her. I spent a lot of time trying to avoid her because from the very first day I didn't want any trouble, but she insisted on provoking a fight with me.

I had struck up a friendship with a Colombiana in for drug traf-ficking, one of many regular female mules that her boyfriend organized in Bogotá, put on the plane with a hundred dollars, and unloaded in Madrid before returning them to Bogotá for their pay. Many of them were caught, since the mule drivers had fingered them to the cops in order to keep the police busy while the other mules passed right under their noses. She was affectionate toward me. She washed my clothes, made my coffee, made my bed. She was one of the protégées that I loved the most and who was the most loyal to me.

The black woman made tea in a small kettle that I used for making coffee. They can take away my water, my blankets, and the sun but not my coffee in the morning. The kettle was broken, and when the Nigerian went to heat water for her tea she spewed insults against us because she thought that we had hidden the kettle. There was no way to calm her down. She hit my protégée. I leapt to her rescue, the other blacks came out fighting, and so did my side. We gave as good as we got, we took out our nails, and, above all, we bit. In prison teeth become a fearful weapon, to the point where a bite from a canine becomes infected if it doesn't get the treatment it deserves. The black woman came up me to take a big bite out of my shoulder, and, as we were lurching around wrapped up like serpents, the "uglies," the riot police, arrived, hitting the two of us with their nightsticks, harassing the others, and bribing the rest. They're animals who rule through hunger, ready to take revenge because everyone—male and female—hates them. The fight was over and the black woman had to start respecting my turf and averting her eyes when I passed.

I came to realize that I had to resign myself to my fate and my punishment the day the high court answered my appeal and gave me eight years, three months, and a day; that is to say, ninety-nine months and a day, or 2,971 days. I acknowledged that I had to pay in full, with every one of the days the judge sentenced me to. I already spent two years in jail and I still dressed as if I were outside, or as if I had just come in: a skirt, a jersey, silk stockings, and heels. I had packed away the uniforms that they gave us and I got choked up and maudlin just looking at them. Sometimes, when I was alone, I put on the blue jeans and the chinos, the maroon shirt buttoned up to the collar, and the tennis shoes, and a chill ran through me, as if I were someone who had just arrived on this planet. I didn't recognize myself, nor did I accept myself dressed like that. I went back to experience the way I lived as a young girl, when they made me feel like an orphan, strange within my own body.

But that day I gave in. I dressed like the prisoners and went out to the patio to see how they looked at me. At first I thought I couldn't do it, that I would start weeping uncontrollably, above all when the others looked at my tiny shoes and the blouse buttoned to the top. Nothing was missing except a haircut and so I got one. I asked permission and I told them to cut it very short. So that no going back was possible. Either I accepted that I was a prisoner or I accepted that I was a prisoner. When I saw myself in the mirror I was totally confused inside, and two tears fell without my even noticing. I brushed them off with my hand, stood in the doorway, thanked the barber, and I was ready: to live without looking backward or inside; to do what I had to without taking myself into consideration. Nothing. Nothing to make me feel better, not even a warm washcloth. Suddenly I saw myself as I was and as I had to be. I accepted it. I did my eight years, three months, and a day. I accepted the uniform of Carabanchel and didn't dwell on the injustice, the judge, or even Antonio.

My daughters were the only thing that mattered to me because I felt that I was robbing them of life, taking their mother away from them. By this time the worst and cruelest things had already happened. The first day, after my call, my brother Carlos had picked them up and brought them to his house. But he didn't have the smarts to think that my arrest was news, and since my daughters were watching television they saw me as the Madrid head of the Medellín cartel, with the coconuts and the cocaine by my side. They grabbed each other and cried without understanding anything of what was going on. Carlos tried to explain it to them and make them feel better, but they wouldn't stop watching television, and the news programs ran the images of Nicanor and myself every hour.

But even so the worst was yet to come. Carlos went to live with a friend and his woman put them up there as well as she could, like poor people: all of them on one sofa. The oldest girl became the mother and she carried the weight of the other two: she washed them, made sure that they ate, prayed alongside them, and tucked them in at night. But the woman was getting on her case and she decided that they weren't to be alone in the house because they made a mess of the place and, what's worse, ate whatever food there was. So, after sending them to off to school at eight in the morning, she took the key and didn't come back to open up for them until seven in the evening, when she returned from work. Which is why I allowed the Mothers' Community of the City of Madrid to take the girls in, even though it was terrible for the them. For sure, the girls didn't tell me what they went through. In the other letter that I received the oldest one wrote me, "Mamá, it's not important to us what you did, the lies they tell don't matter, we only want to know what happened as you tell it. No one else can tell us. Tell us what's true and what's a lie; tell us yes or no, but *you* tell us. You do everything well, you do it for us, you do it because you have to. Tell us what you want, but *you* tell us. Don't worry about us, we know how to do what you taught us and we will be waiting for you the day they set you free."

I believe I had accepted that jail was a brief rest, as it was for all the women who suffered alongside me. I also accepted that I needed tenderness, that I needed someone to caress me, because solitude rubs your skin raw and gives you a pain that won't let you live. I let other inmates get closer to me to ask who I was, what I had done, who I loved; I accepted that I was alone and that I needed others who would look after me and watch over me, because all of us were prisoners.

During that time a large van arrived from the airport: fifteen young girls who had been grabbed off two flights, one Iberia and the other Avianca. They were caught almost at once; they came ratted on from Bogotá. All of the women with the cookies in their stomachs, all of them less than twenty years old, all of them with five hundred dollars in their purse. They arrived crying, with their noses red from so much sniffling. You could see them crying day and night, as if they were gypsies. Some were from Pereira and others from Cúcuta; there were three women from Bogotá and two from Los Llanos. All of them innocent and "without breakfast."[5] The one who had recruited them, pissed off because of a job that turned out badly, had informed on the entire group. He contacted the police by phone and told them everything, with a thousand details. Surrounded when they were seized, they were taken to the Plaza de Castilla around midnight, and then the problem came up: none of them wanted to flush out the cookies. None of them accepted the "treatment." Logical, inasmuch as the treatment they give to force out the contraband that you carry inside is nasty and degrading.

Among them there was a quiet girl with flashing eyes and a small body: her name was Dianita. She was the only one who wasn't making a scene, wasn't carrying on about the injustice in a loud voice, wasn't crying all day.

I watched her from a distance and up close, I talked to her without hitting on her; I combed her long, black hair while she told me that she had gotten involved in smuggling because she wanted to study medicine. She'd finished college, graduating with an excellent grade point average at Javeriana University, but she didn't have the means to study further. A friend introduced her to another friend who knew somebody that proposed the trip to her; she accepted the offer and got on board. But she didn't weep. I invited her to stay with me in the

But living and not turned into a vegetable, like those who ended up in psychiatric. That's where they took the ones who were running on the roof or whose screws were loose, and from there no one returns. Blondie Mallarino stayed there, a high-class girl who was caught at the airport with her skis full of coke. She was a really good-looking woman, well-bred, spoke English, French, and Italian; her uncles worked in the Ministry of Foreign Affairs and the family were ambassadors by trade. She was in love with an American from New York; they skied together at the best resorts during the winter and in the summer they went from casino to casino and island to island in a sailboat.

They traveled to Colombia to ski in the Ruiz Mountain Range and to meet her family in Bogotá. They were there twenty days, a month, and then he left for New York in order to meet her later in Madrid. He left his skis behind for Blondie to bring and that's how it went down: she was caught at Barajas. One kilo of crystal cocaine in each ski: eight years, three months, and a day.

Blondie walked in looking over her shoulder; she was gruff and didn't stoop to talk to anyone. She kept to herself; she didn't eat, and she didn't lie down on the bed but instead spent the whole night sitting on the pillow. She showered every time they let her because everything, everything, filled her with disgust; she believed that the prison was a nest of AIDS and she didn't even touch the walls. We women tried to warn her, but she didn't listen; she said "thank you" without being thankful to us, and of course she didn't listen to us at all.

And so the days went by. As far as she was concerned, everything had a bad odor. She was given to saying that it smelled of cat shit. She was obsessed by this odor, she smelled it everywhere. She sniffed her hands and her clothes; she spent her time smelling the nooks and crannies, trying to find the cat that was making her life impossible. It wasn't worth it to talk to her and explain that in Carabanchel there were neither toms nor bitches, nor any animals at all. She was adamant about the odor of cat shit. It harassed her everywhere, and when she sat on her bed one night and began to hiss as if she herself were a cat in heat, we knew that she had gone mad. But not yet. She was still shy dormitory and, since I could, I asked my protégée if she would switch her bed while Dianita settled in. I explained to her, like she was one of my daughters, the way they ran the cellblocks, El Tigre,[6] the courtyards, work. She was a child in my eyes; I watched out for her, and where she looked I looked there too. I needed a reason to go on living my 2,971 days; we shared every intimacy and wore each other's clothes; hearing her breathe during the night gave me all the strength the two of us needed to live through the day; to open my eyes by her side was to live on a promise; to shelter her with my body was to fly as one.

We went out to work at our jobs at eight thirty in the morning and only at the two thirty mealtime did we come in contact again. Then we were apart until eight thirty in the evening; she ate quickly and went to the cellblock to make my coffee and fix my bed. Her friends were getting to know me and little by little we were making the whole cellblock ours, until it was only Colombian women living there. We became very strong and not only ran the dormitory but little by little the kitchens, the bathrooms, the visiting room, and the workshops. The peasants—as Dianita used to say—ended up shifting the gears. We forced the Nigerians, the gypsies, and the Andalusians to accept discipline and order. We gave orders because we knew how to make ourselves into a force in whatever area, we were faithful to each other unto death, and, since we knew how to lay down the law, even the officials and the guards respected us.

None of the Colombian women went to the punishment cell, and, if any of us ever saw it, it was only because we cleaned it up. More than anyone else it was the Andalusians, who acted like newborn goddesses, who were thrown there. Solitary is a room without windows where you can't even hear the slightest noise: it's like a thermos. One week, two, three, five, and when you come back you won't recognize or know anyone. They shove your food in through a hole in the door and every twelve hours you have the right to an hour in an isolated courtyard, where no one can speak with anyone else, no one looks at you, no one even crosses paths. You go into solitary screaming and come out quiet.

of the mark: she went into the hospital and we began to hear shouts, grating outbursts. We went to look at what was going on. Blondie shouted that she had defecated cat shit. She pointed at it while she was shouting. We carefully carried her out and comforted her. We knew that they were going to take her to psychiatric. And so she went. They tied her up, carried her off, and put her to sleep with barbiturates. The treatment is simple and cruel: pills. The women become things, vegetables. At first they sleep, then they stop sleeping, they don't cry, until they sit there with their eyes wide open. Some of the women die right there, others they release to die outside.

I was only twenty days short of finishing my 2,971 when Doña Carmen came in. I didn't know her very well, but her story seems to me the saddest of all. She is a campesina from Tolima who experienced the violence in Rovira from when she was very little. She was never able to shake off what she saw in her dreams and so she was always in pain. When she was an adult she had twins, a pair of beautiful daughters who were the light of her life. But one of the two was born with a weak heart. She had a defective valve. It wasn't open when she was born and for that reason her heart didn't beat regularly, sufficient blood didn't get to the brain, and the little girl was partially retarded.

She started to look desperately for a doctor, a medicine man, or a witch doctor who could help her. She went to the Children's Hospital, to Children's Heart, to the Samaritan; she went where the saintly doctor José Gregorio Hernández had lived and even went to Putamayo looking for a shaman. No luck. It was a question of an operation with a knife, and the doctors in Colombia don't have mercy on anyone. In the Palermo Clinic she met an attentive young doctor who promised to help her. "I can't help you, señora," he said, "But I know someone who will loan you the money for the operation." Happy and ready to do anything, she agreed to talk to the man who knew what to do to get hold of the money. The man explained to her that it was a question of carrying a package to Madrid, that it would pay ten thousand dollars. Carmen accepted the job happily because that was more or less what was needed for the girl's operation. He explained to her that the "favor" was simple: deliver a suitcase to Prado del Principe Street, number 508, in Madrid. Nothing else. They gave her half the money at El Dorado Airport so that she could give it to the doctor who was going to operate on the girl, and the other half when she returned, so she could take the girl out of the clinic. She perhaps distrusted not so much the suitcase but rather that the doctors would perform the correct operation on her daughter and not something else. That's what tormented her. She didn't want to think why she was carrying the suitcase in order to deliver it, although, since she was a pretty desperate woman, she should have figured it out. But what could she do? They handed her the suitcase, gave her two hundred dollars change on top of the five thousand, which in reality the doctor received, and she got on the plane. She arrived in Madrid with her humble face, in her working woman's Sunday best, and of course they grabbed her. She went through customs, headed out of the airport, hailed a cab that took her directly to Plaza de Castilla, where the Guardia Civil was waiting for her with everything ready. She was immediately arrested.

From the time she arrived and found out that she could work, she dedicated herself to doing everything she could do and everything she couldn't. She was wide-awake, a woman on the move. I never saw her cry even once. She went looking for money everywhere. She took care of other people's beds, she shined their shoes, cleaned the bathrooms, sewed clothing. She saved so she could pay the doctor the rest of what she owed for the operation. To get five thousand dollars together in Carabanchel isn't easy. To tell the truth, it's almost impossible.

I later learned that she didn't manage to deliver the money that was needed because the little girl died. She didn't give up in despair but instead pushed for the other twin to join her. The Mothers' Community was taking care of her. I knew her. She was a beautiful and very sweet girl. When I got out I brought her to live with me at my apartment for a few weekends and my daughters adored her like a small toy.

I believe that one of the hardest things in jail are the last days. Time doesn't pass, it stays wrapped up in the hours, there are snarls from one minute to the next, and it never arrives anywhere. You go about arranging the valise you are taking with you, putting everything in its place and making a long list of the things you are going to leave behind, for whom and why. You look back at this one's behavior and that one's, their tastes and their fondness, and you go on distributing: the mascara for Alicia, who gave me the yogurt at breakfast; the green scarf for María, who called for me to go to the visitation room when my daughters arrived; the slippers to Virginia, because one time she said to me that they looked comfortable; the alarm clock to Helena, who always overslept; and everything else for Diana. For Dianita I left everything that I'd come to love: my white sneakers, my fancy earrings, a book of Neruda's love poems, and a devil carved in wood, which was my pet object and the handkerchief for my tears.

The hour of leaving went on for ever. They didn't come for me, the padlocks on the doors didn't make a sound; nobody shows up and you're shivering. The last twenty minutes I lived one by one; if you lived your whole life like that, it would last almost forever. Until finally the door to the prison wing clatters open and the cell door creaks and the order of liberty is given. And then the tiny steps, the good-byes, the places you passed through, where you lived and wept, the courtyards, the warden's office, the jokes, the documents stamped, the slaps on the back, the promise "Never again," the clothes and the things that they had confiscated from you when you arrived, and, finally, the door, the enormous light, the open spaces, and my daughters waiting for me in a taxi.

We got into the car in the middle of kisses and tears and, just when we were going down the avenue, I saw Antonio, the Argentine, out of the corner of my eye. I had made up my mind to kill him because his testimony sank me. The DA used it as conclusive evidence, and the judge accepted it as such. It was he who I called from jail to pick up my daughters and take care of them, above all the youngest, so that when she left the day care she wasn't run over by a car. The police followed, detained, and interrogated him, and he confessed that I had told him those coconuts were full of cocaine and that I had asked his help in selling them. The only thing the DA needed to convict me was some proof, as small as it was, that I really knew what the coconuts had inside them, that I was aware and therefore was part of the Medellín cartel. Let the truth be told: when I discovered that there weren't six thousand coconuts but a whole container ship with thirty two thousand on board, I started to suspect that they had to have something valuable inside. But in spite of that I kept going—a really naive woman—making contacts at Corte Inglés to sell them. The suspicion grew more vivid when Germán asked me to let him make a call to Colombia from my telephone. The conversation concerned surgery he was going to have in Barcelona and, as soon as he was "back to health," that he was going to call again. The surgery was, obviously, the arrival of the coconuts. I called Antonio, told him everything, said to him that I thought those coconuts weren't so coconut, that my feminine intuition told me that they were hiding something because they never have to operate on a man in good health for no reason, even if he is fifty years old, and that no one is going to risk bringing thirty-two thousand coconuts without having a contract to sell them in advance. That's as far as my chitchat and my fear went. From there on out the rest—the part that condemned me—Antonio put in, adding that I knowingly had decided to take possession of the coconuts. The real truth—I'm saying it now—is that I didn't know, I only had the suspicion.

Coming out of Carabanchel I saw him, waiting to see that they had released me. I wanted to get out of the car and tear his eyes out, but I was so happy crying with my daughters that I didn't want to interrupt an embrace that I was ready to hold on to for eight years, three months, and a day but that I paid for with only thirty eight months: eleven hundred forty days and nights.

Sharon's Diary

June 21, 10 P.M.

I've decided to write this diary because I know that what is going to happen will never happen again. You never repeat anything, even if you spend your whole life doing the same thing. But right now I have the feeling, the certainty, that I am about to live something that I can't put aside, like so many things that end up swallowed by time.

We traveled for two hours in canoes loaded down with six thousand pounds of the best herb—the fattest buds, the best tips, and the fewest seeds—that we could find in La Reserva, a small village in San Pedro de la Sierra where there are a more than a hundred sanctuaries, a good number of pressers, and many growers. Marimba's real owner is he who knows how to defend his crop with bullets.[1] Everything else is just a bunch of white lies. Five gunmen were hired to get it, although in truth I have to say that she paid Ñito Argüelles, a native of Ciénaga, in cash without a fuss. Ñito has been in trouble with the Cárdenas from the day he found himself forced to sell the whole stash he'd hidden in San Javier to the Baldeblánquez.

It's a dispute that goes way back and that won't be over until both sides have finished each other off. If there is one still alive, whatever side he's on, the bullets will fly on the dance floor. Because it was at a dance that things started. In San Antonio, above Dibulla, Toño Cardenas, a big man, quiet and honest, didn't want his girlfriend to dance with Juanito Baldeblánquez because he didn't. He didn't give him the reason, and actually they were cousins and the closest of friends. They went on many escapades together, drank for three days without separating, played dominoes, and knew each other's thousand secrets. But they met their fate flashing in Celmira's eyes. She was indeed beautiful, although I think that they loved her less than they put on and boast about. There was greater fame in not letting the other have her than in having her. They say that Juanito was the more adamant, Celmira being Toño's girlfriend. The atmosphere became dangerous when everybody saw Juanito's insistence. Toño gave up several times and even acted ignorant when Juanito took his girlfriend out to dance one time, and then another and another. But when Toño didn't want to give him room to take her out to dance again, Juanito went to peel out his 38, and the other, who was more of a fighter, shot him dead without a word.

Wars between families are sacred; they don't recognize truces because they spring from the blood of rivals. The worst enemy is the one who can't forget.

I'm writing quickly so as not to let fear get inside me and open the door to my wound. The lights of the airport, the flashing green and yellow of the tower, must be guiding Jim toward us. Nacha went with me to pick the best herb. We went from one side of the zone to the other, smoking and sniffing all the different qualities, until we'd tasted everything there was. She is well versed on what gets exported from these parts and what they ask for up North.

I told her I didn't like her name because it struck me as hard. "Don't worry about it, call me whatever you want: Cacha, Perla, Aguadija.[2] When I was baptized they named me María Ignacia. María for the Virgin; Ignacia for San Ignacio de Loyola," and she started to tell me the story of her life. Little by little, between silences as we climbed the hills looking for the best herb, shouting as we ran down grabbing onto the steep slopes, or talking when we sat down to let our sweat cool off.

Nacha doesn't know where or who gave birth to her. She considers herself a "stepchild," as they say in the Sierra. At thirteen years old she had weeping fits that didn't stop for fiestas, expeditions, or boyfriends. Her mother Doña Carlota thought she had come of age and said as much to the whole world. Nacha herself didn't know why she cried so much or where those lonely torrents that ran down her cheeks came from. But one day during Christmastime her cousins came to spend the holidays, and, without knowing why, she asked Juan Darío, the oldest and cockiest of her cousins, what they said about her, María

Ignacia, during the trip between Medellín and Barranquilla. Nacha told me that the question had came out of the same place where the tears came from but that she never could explain to herself why she had asked Juan Darío. What happened was, the brat's expression changed, he became afraid and, without hesitating, he said,"You aren't your mother's daughter; you're adopted." The flood of tears stopped immediately. On that day she opened her investigation and began to retrieve memories from that hazy region that was her childhood.

She remembered playing ball in a courtyard—which she later learned was the Orphanage of San José—with the Sisters of the Poor. There were other girls the same age and dressed like she was, all of them in white—shoes, aprons, and diadem—but when the week started they changed into a dark blue uniform. She loved Mother Assumption most of all, because she kissed her until she fell asleep and because her habit didn't smell of smoke from candles or of mothballs.

The day she had her first period Doña Carlota told her while she got dressed that Mother Assumption was Piedad's sister. "Piedad's your real mother, a beautiful woman who left you in the care of your aunt because she hadn't married your father; nobody knew who he was, although I was able to figure out that he is none other than Alberto de la Rosa himself, a very rich man but a big coward, on account of his being one of the better people in Barranquilla. I say this because he has your same droopy eyes, which made him so popular during the annual Carnivals."

While she told me so many intimacies—for no reason at all, since we had just gotten to know each other climbing the mountains—I thought that she must have changed her name because this Nacha was very hard and was liable to be confused with macha, cacha, tacha.[3] But I couldn't figure out what to call her. She understood and told me, "Call me whatever you like; for my part I like my name exactly because it's confusing and it embarrasses people to call me that. The nuns called me a thousand different names: Encarnación, Expiación, and at times even San Miguel, San Nicolás, San Eufracio."

11 P.M.

No sign of Jim. The night was full of stars, but the horizon remained dark and there was nothing to cure me of the anxiety of waiting. Nacha says to me that the *Rochi*—the *Locust*—the boat where we are going to load the shipment, could be delayed but would arrive before dawn. Jim has never missed an appointment with anyone. The son of Scots, he knows how to keep his word despite wind and high tides.

Jim is a sailor who has experience of the ocean because he was born near the water's edge, on an island in the Canadian Pacific north of Vancouver called Little Wifey. A green island in the summer and white in the winter, with just one house on it, his parent's, where his mother still lives today. When he was very young his uncle Tom took him out to the docks where, running around first and working later, he learned all the secrets of cod fishing. He also learned how to play cards and billiards and he became as well known in King as in Three Bands. One night he won enough money playing dirty poker with some inebriated Japanese to go in with Larry, his childhood friend, on the purchase of a small fishing boat. Nacha says that at the beginning they weren't convinced about fishing and taking care of the boat. They headed out to the open sea with provisions for three months and came back with the freezer full of cod. They sold the fish in half an hour and stayed on land long enough to screw around with the whores, buy equipment, and repair the boat.

At first, when the friends got back together after ten years of not seeing each other—Larry was a whaler in the Pacific, a mercenary in Africa, an opium trafficker in Thailand—Jim was all ears. They got up before dawn, threw out the nets, and got drunk while talking about everything under the sun; in the afternoon they pulled in the nets, put the fish in the freezer, and went back to getting drunk. So great was Jim's passion for listening to Larry that when they were back on dry land he followed after him to the point of sleeping in the same bed in which the other guy was stretched out with a prostitute; they ended up sleeping with two—and even with four—women at the same time. They went their separate ways only to visit their mothers, because that is an intimacy that the Canadians—as cold as their oceans—don't share.

Nacha—or Pearl, as I am starting to call her—just finished telling me that she thought she saw a light moving, one that didn't seem to be a shooting star. Without knowing much about stars, I also believe I saw something move, very far away. A few minutes have gone by and the light shows up, larger this time. There's no doubt: it's a boat.

Larry and Jim got back together again, boarded the ship, and went back to getting drunk as if they hadn't seen each other for another ten years. But with time they were speaking less and less. Each trip they played cards or dominoes more often and passed more time putting together ten-thousand-piece jigsaw puzzles. On dry land both of them shut themselves up for three or four days with their call girl—or call girls—until the day arrived to say good-bye to their mothers and head back to the boat. There they would say hello to each other and set to work, each one doing the job that fell to him, without exchanging a word. Like that for three months. Jim decided to sell his part to Larry because the silence, the cold, and, above all—above all, Pearl insisted—because he would awake in the night with a shout, certain that a large cruise ship had hit them and destroyed the boat. The dream was becoming stronger and more real every night until Jim was so afraid of sleeping that he became addicted to caffeine, to Benzedrine, and finally to cocaine. The day came when Jim couldn't sleep without a bottle of calvados, a French brandy that he left lying around in his bunk.

Pearl just shouted at me from the beach that for real the light is from the *Rochi* and we should prepare the canoes so we can make the shipment. The night is as placid as the sea.

Jim invited me to join them on board until they load the marimba onto a mother ship that will meet up with us fifty miles off the east coast of Florida. I accepted, making it clear that my work went up to the point where the herb was loaded onto the sailboat and once I had been paid the amount we agreed on.

The *Rochi* is a fifty-foot sailboat with two masts, a Loran (a navigational tool), a Deep Founder (to measure ocean depth), an automatic pilot so you can sleep, and a fifty-watt radio. It was built in Taiwan of teak and fiberglass; it has a hold that can accommodate six thousand pounds of herb, leaving only a bunk free for Jim, Pearl, Dodge, an islander from Providencia who takes the second watch on board, and myself to sleep in. I told Jim that I have sailed many times, although I have to confess that I was only out on the sea when I was fifteen.

June 22

It's six in the morning. Everyone is asleep. As soon as Jim guided his *Rochi* to the open sea and fixed the course, he went to sleep. I watched him for a good while to see if he got in bed with Perla, until I calmed down. I slept all night to the lullaby of the ship's swaying. She sleeps naked on top of the covers. I would like it more if she were named Carolina and she slept with her clothes on. She has a small body, soft, that looks like it was made from the wood of the Guayacan, with a deep space between her breasts as if she were missing a bone. Her breath is soft, coming from another world, and it just barely moves the little hairs on her upper lip. She opens her eyes and looks at me. She closes them again as if forgiving me and then turns face downward; she knows she is desired, and she has become accustomed to getting around what others expect from her from the time when she was working on her bachelor's degree and she threw her school uniform into the hamper, put on some blue jeans and sandals, and went by herself to the Woodstock that Jota Mario Arbeláez organized in La Estrella. It was a copy of the real one. From that day she was no longer the same person. She knew what it was to walk with her feet on the ground and she didn't concern herself again with grade books. She tried maracachafa, as the country folk call weed,[4] and she became a frequent visitor to the Antioquia neighborhood, where all the dealers gave her a bag just to get a good look at her.

A little earlier they had expelled her from the Salesian Mothers' School because the rector considered her to be the bad apple who stirred up trouble in class. In reality the chain of responsibility started with another schoolmate named Álvarez who not only was the first name to be called but also the first on line and the head of the class. She had gotten hold of the telephone number for one of the most well-known bordellos in Medellín, known as Bucarelia. The crime consisted in calling up on the phone, listening, answering, and hanging up; calling again later, asking for Nelly and hanging up; then talking to Nelly, and, finally, asking her about the man she liked the most. The mother superior found out everything and put the blame on Perla because of who she was—all the nuns knew it—and because the other school girls had influential parents in Medellín. But for Perla that event, without ever accepting her responsibility, opened a door for her to another world. She continued her studies at Conrado González School and later at the business academy; then she traveled to the United States on vacation. When she came back she spoke English and had been reading Henry Miller's *Tropic of Cancer*.

7 A.M.

They're starting to wake up little by little. Everyone's thirsty because last night, after loading the marimba on board, we drank two bottles of Caña rum. Dodge just let out a shout: "There's no drinking water!" Jim runs to take a look and, sure enough, one of the crates of marimba was unloaded right on top of the water pipes and it broke one. There's no drinking water! All we have is the water in the toilets, which is to say three liters. Perla isn't bothered, and I, as happens to me when heavy things take place, I laugh with a laugh that sometimes ends up making me cry. "Son of a bitch," Jim says looking at us all one by one. "We are out of water!"

There's nothing to be done. Either we go back or we keep going. The desalination pump that we brought with us only makes one bottle every twenty-four hours. Which means: check your thirst and pray. Perla, who is the one who knows about saints, tell us that San Isidro makes many miracles, but on dry land, and that Santa Bárbara only guards against storms on the high seas. We remain silent until Jim says, "We're going to keep going. Everyone is allowed two sips of water daily, and everybody has to keep busy—preferably in the shade—doing something so they don't go crazy. The sails have to be patched, the hemp and cotton have to be threaded to make rope, and we can play dominoes. We'll take turns on the rudder every two hours. The food will be a little saltier than usual, and we'll only eat once a day. I calculate that if we make good time we'll arrive at our destination in six days."

Dodge, a corpulent black guy six feet tall, protests that he thinks the water ration shouldn't be the same for everyone and proposes that it be proportional to size. Perla realizes she's being referred to, understands what he means, and shoots back at the big shit. "Black son of a bitch, what have you got against me? I'll say it straight out, you're starting a fight with me. Take all the water you want, I know who has the biggest balls in the game you're playing. Can I start my shift on the tiller?" she asked Jim, leaving Dodge with his jaw hanging open.

From the cabin I watch Perla moving the tiller with her hair blowing free in the wind. Brown hair with red highlights when the sun shines on it. Sometimes she puts it in one braid, other times two, and when she is busy and intent she gathers it in a bun that she puts up with a pencil. Last night she told me she had met Jim in Mexico City, in Plaza Coyoacán on a Sunday afternoon, listening to an amateur sing "Ojitos Tapatíos" for free,[5] along with other songs that amateur singers learn in order to make a name for themselves. Jim stood by her side listening and suddenly, without a word or a gesture, they were leaning on each other. They walked together holding hands looking at the acrobats, jugglers, dancers, necklace and kite sellers, and the people. The people who walked around—like they did—carefree. They went to the house where Rivera lived with Frida Kahlo without speaking and without her knowing who this extremely tall gringo with a ponytail and two earrings in his left ear was. He had spent eight months learning Spanish and he spoke almost perfectly. They ended up in Plaza Garibaldi, drunk, listening to every song by José Alfredo Jiménez, and they made love that night, the night after, and the night after, until they ended up living together.

What money Jim still had from the fishing boat he wanted to invest in a sailboat equipped to search for Spanish galleons and German submarines. But it was too expensive. The dollars he had barely gave him enough to buy the *Rochi*. He had read everything there was about the treasure of the Atocha; he knew exactly where it had sunk, the amount of gold it carried, and even the crew members' names. He spent hours explaining to Perla how it sank and how the treasure could be rescued. That was where the idea for the trip we were on came from.

Over a long period of time Jim had saved all the money to buy the boat that could raise the Atocha. He didn't waste even a penny from that account and, for that reason, he had to work. He did everything: he was a barber and a masseur, a tailor and a mechanic. They lived in Tepoztlán, letting themselves float away on the dreams they were constructing bit by bit. The undertaking consisted in making a shipment of marijuana from Colombia to the United States and, with the money, buying a ship to haul out the treasure. They climbed up Teposteco hill to watch the sunsets and came down to eat after it was already nighttime.

One day the circus came to town and the two, in love as they were, took seats in the front row. In order to perform the knives of fire routine, Ruth the Redskin asked for a volunteer who wanted to put himself in the center of the target. Jim was born to play that role. In order to kill time and keep the audience's attention, Ruth started asking him dumb questions, his tongue got twisted, and out of fear he answered almost completely in English, while the audience laughed and laughed until they ended up applauding for him without his needing to perform the knives of fire act. The show belonged so much to Jim that the owner of the circus hired him to make people laugh. A little later he confessed to Perla that he was in love with Ruth and that he was going to tour with the circus in Chiapas and Guatemala.

Perla stayed a few more days in Mexico and went back to Medellín. But she didn't abandon their project, and she came right back to look for ways to be involved in the business. Just the same, in Medellín she wasn't well-known and the Antioquians didn't know about anything except marijuana. She wanted to get involved in cocaine.

Dodge just called us to eat: canned beans and rice with coconut. Perla got on his case for not saving the water from the coconuts for drinking and he told her to go to hell. My thirst is making me scared. Jim says that the thing that can screw us—if we let it—is the agony of knowing we are without water and not thirst itself.

June 23

It's four in the afternoon. It's been a quiet day. I've passed the time looking at María—as I'm calling Perla today—sew the sails. She has long fingers that weave rapidly. In this respect the nuns didn't waste their time. She seems accustomed to navigate through her dreams staring at the point of the needle. I write and I look at her. Up on deck Jim is fishing and he has promised us a whippet to eat; Dodge stares at him from his turn at the tiller just as I look at María.

Toward evening we listen hopefully to a storm drawing close, we get all the cans and pots ready to collect fresh water, we even made a receptacle with a sail. We wait and we wait but the clouds don't want to come close. I notice that María is, for the first time, agitated; she has gone back to walking around in sandals, as if she were on dry land. She is reading *My Life* by Isadora Duncan.

June 24

Eleven in the morning. We sail and sail. The sky is overcast, but it doesn't rain. The rain is uppermost in everyone's mind. María has gone back to mending the ropes and she taught me how: you undo the parts that are worn down, untwist each strand some eight inches, and then braid the ends around each other again. María said to me that these braids, once they're made, never become broken. She looks at me for a long time silently. A chill runs through me from my head to my feet, like last night's storm that never arrived. I sit by her side braiding the ropes, sensing her without looking at her. I've taken a liking to the strange mood that lies behind her silence.

For breakfast Dodge serves us peanuts with raisins, cashews, and nuts. In the afternoon María taught me to make sailors' knots. She was a good teacher, but a bit of a tyrant. She was irritated when I got lost and didn't know what to do next and she ended up yelling at me. Jim, who was sitting next to her reading, looked at me and smiled, somewhere between maliciously and condescendingly.

It's four in the afternoon now. The storm that came up to flirt with us is drawing close once again. Today I'm sure that we are going to have water to drink again, to bathe ourselves, and to throw the fear of dying of thirst overboard. Once again everything is ready. María walks around in her bare feet again. I notice that she has a corns between the fourth and fifth toes on both feet.

The first drops start to fall when the sun has finished its day's work. They are big drops that fall angrily and nearly make a puddle on top of the sea. We all behold the happiness in each other's eyes, stripping off our clothes as the rain grows heavier. We open our hands, legs, and mouths, attempting to let the rainwater get as far into us as the thirst did. Dodge sings a hallelujah, which sounds out of place. At such times you feel like a film star shooting a film about yourself. Jim dedicates himself to making sure that the receptacle made out of sails doesn't fall apart, while María lets her hair down. I can't stop looking at her.

The downpour lasts for more than an hour. Time enough for us to bathe and get rid of everything that had accumulated between our breasts and our backs over four nights. We drank all the water that we could gather up in our hands while Dodge promised to cook us a run-down, shark in coconut, that very night.

María turned me on to Keith Jarret, teaching me to feel his piano coming from so far away, so passionate in his search, so full of colors and silence. She eats without saying a word, very attentive to what she is doing. In the orphanage she ate alone. Not at the wooden tables, where the poor orphans took their meals, or in the refectory, where the sisters ate. When all was said and done, she was the adopted daughter of the mother superior and the apple of the eye of all the nuns except one, Sister Eleuteria, a tall woman with severe eyes who meted out punishment with a leather strap she carried in the pocket of her habit. María hid under a piece of furniture when the sister came in and she stayed there staring at her black shoes with their rubber soles. She only breathed again when they moved away, squeaking on the always shiny floors of the orphanage.

The corridors of the orphanage surrounded a patio full of flowers where there was a grotto dedicated to the Virgin of Fatima, with little shepherds and sheep. The place gave María a feeling of safety and above all happiness, because that was where she was on the day that a tall man with green eyes knocked on the door of the convent, bringing her a chain tricycle wrapped in cellophane paper. Mother Asunción explained to her that he was a "benefactor," and, years later, when María was in school, she confessed that that person, the first man that María knew, was her uncle, brother of the nun who was her real mother. But from that moment she thought that her benefactor was her real father.

María lived with the nuns until the days when, crying, she said to Mother Asunción that she wanted a "wealthy mommy." She was five years old and she surely had seen the ladies who came to visit the orphanage. A rich and well-known Medellín family took her on as a daughter and gave her the affection that she needed.

June 25

We have tacked a few degrees to the east so we can pass between the Dominican Republic and Puerto Rico, a more secure route than by the Mona Channel, which is usually watched closely by Cuban ships.[6] We are sailing along happily because the wind is strong and there is enough water. María is going barefoot again and she is more beautiful and prouder than ever. I suspect that she stopped loving Jim some time ago and that they now maintain a merely professional relationship.

In Mexico María had decided to make money, a lot of money, in any way she could, and there's only one way everybody knows. When she left the house she made a promise to herself to live life on her own and not return to her parents and, for that reason, she didn't go back to Medellín but instead set herself up in Bogotá. She arrived determined to move ahead on the plan of making the shipment.

The first thing she proposed to do was to make contact with a "line," a network for which she needed to locate a dealer who sold high-quality merchandise. She knew that on Seventh Avenue, from San Diego Park to the Bank of the Republic, there were vendors who happened on the "monkeys" who went around looking for them. She dressed up like a gringa: she changed the color of her hair, bought a large flower print dress, put on dark glasses, and went out to Seventh. She felt a little like a prostitute, a little like a detective, and a little like bait. And finally one came up to her, but the coke was greasy and yellowish. She didn't like it. She rejected two, three, and four dealers with the same quality. But she remained determined to find what she was looking for.

One afternoon she was sitting in the Florida cafeteria eating chocolate when a young woman sat down at her table and, without further ado, said, "I have what you want." She lived on Fifth Avenue at 23d, and there, in her apartment, she laid out on the table five types of coke, all very fine, for María to choose from. She selected a pure crystal and bought twenty grams, which was her reserve to start the business. In the hotel where she was living she cut the wrapping paper and made fifty portions, which she wrapped carefully in the soft white paper. She put five in her handbag and just like that she went to open her market north of Bogotá, where nobody knew her and she could pass, given her hair color, for a girl from a good family. In one night she sold all fifty packages and went back to her friend to buy more.

The dealer's name was Berta and she was, like María, from Antioquia. Straightforward, with a sunny disposition, she always went about taking care of business.

She made each move with great care, she found the quality that people asked her for and in the quantity that was available. María was part of the network and not just the merchandise. For that reason she saved all—or nearly all—she earned to add to the reserve and to give Berta confidence. After a few days she moved out of her hotel for an apartment close to her friend. Berta was sometimes too kind, calling her "my queen."

María accepted the role and they became close friends. They were known as "the earrings," because they always went around together.

One afternoon Berta came to María's apartment in tears. They had caught up with her and she had to get lost. The police had her in their grasp. It was the moment that María was waiting for; furthermore, she could have turned her in so that Berta would have been forced to pass the network on to her, but since she felt a sincere friendship and she had even come to love her, the temptation was nothing more than an evil whim. María offered to hide her and Berta gratefully opened up with all the information. The connections to the laboratories on one side and the ties to the mules and the contacts in Los Angeles on the other. In reality they had formed an export business, with María in charge and Berta behind the scenes. But since the "hits" from the police were so strong and persistent, María was left to pull all the strings while Berta was, little by little, isolated and a prisoner of security measures.

Buying the merchandise from the laboratories didn't present any problems. They would ask for the quantities needed to make the "pastries" or to load up the mules, requests that were first sent in from outside the country. María became the highest-priced pastrymaker in the routes headed to Los Angeles, Mexico, and New York. She layered false bottoms in suitcases, books, stacks of magazines, shoes, umbrellas, luggage carriers.

She succeeded in making a paste from a base of glue and sulfur that threw the dogs off the scent. She handled everything and didn't let anyone else get involved, more because of security than ambition. Her shipments were never intercepted.

More difficult and delicate was the management of the mules. She had to start by picking them out, testing them, then loading them up, and finally getting them back. María went out to look for young men and women between eighteen and twenty-five years old. She found them in the bars, on the streets, in the parks. She analyzed them carefully: their clothes, manners, conversation. She didn't want ordinary mules but rather exceptional ones: she had decided to choose her own secure team. The best place to locate the candidates was the Colombo-Americano. Young people, serious, ambitious and, above all, admirers of the United States. Her cover was easy: to practice her English. She was putting together a team of five: two women and three men. She went about letting them know what she was doing and she didn't choose those who said "yes" but those who said "yes, but . . ." They were more trustworthy and reliable. She first instructed the baby mules on the trip: airports, customs, airplanes, food, conversations with other passengers, and relations with the stewardesses; then on how to handle their stomachs, distress, ambition, money. She spent whole days explaining the details and listening to their reactions until finally she chose two: a man and a woman.

Berta had taught her the methods for loading the mules through the mouth, but with a doctor friend María discovered that the acids in the large intestine were gentler than in the small intestine or in the stomach itself, and she made up her mind to load them through their tails.

Two days before the flight she hid the two baby mules with their suitcases ready, their passports and their money. They read, watched television, and gabbed. They weren't able to eat anything but chicken soup, along with booster shots of serum and vitamins that she gave them. She cleaned out their stomachs with soap, and six hours before the trip, she started to load them from behind with little balls of cocaine wrapped up in condoms. Each one weighed ten grams. The girl was able to take on eighty five of them and the boy, who was bigger and stronger, one hundred and twenty two. Loaded up, out to the airport; then on to the plane and later to Los Angeles via Mexico on Mexicana Airlines.

In Los Angeles they were met by one of Jim's brothers with whom María had worked out the business. "A reliable little monkey," she said. He unpacked the mules and he also brought them back to health with serum and vitamins over the course of two days, until they were able to go out onto the street with fifty dollars each, just to take a look around. After eight days they were on their way back.

They never grabbed even one of María's mules. She made money on this job, but she wanted to send a large shipment "to know once and for all if I get rich or am going to go through my whole life fucked."

June 26, 4 P.M.

We heard over the radio that a storm with potential to become a hurricane is forming to the east of Puerto Rico. Jim told us that the news is serious because we would have to veer to the west to pass through the Mona Channel, more protected and dangerous than the open sea to the east of Puerto Rico.

6 P.M.

News of the hurricane is confirmed. They've named it David and say it's already traveling at sixty miles an hour. Jim points out the utter tranquillity of the ocean where we are, at the border between Haiti and the Dominican Republic. There isn't even a little breeze. The *Rochi* has come to a complete halt; the ripples on the surface are barely visible; a fearful silence surrounds us. Everything is quiet. Only the setting sun is moving. Jim explains to us that the hurricane is sucking up all the energy from this part of the planet and that this is what is known as *calma chicha*, total calm. Night is coming on, exaggerating the silence, the stillness, and the fear. The little thirty horsepower engine barely moves the *Rochi*. The sails don't do anything at all; we are beached in the middle of the Caribbean and threatened by a hurricane, far from the coast. Dodge has put on a life jacket, and María her sandals. María has the virtue of making my fears go away when she puts her shoes on and giving me strength when she is quiet. Jim is on deck looking into the distance and "sniffing" the air. I feel useless in this dangerous moment. We are practically drifting. The little motor struggles against the law of gravity without much success. I listen to its superhuman effort and it gives me a feeling of tenderness to hear it battle on alone.

June 27

The night passes in the same stillness that it began. The wind continues to hide, nothing ruffles the waves, there's not even one seagull from all those that traveled with us. Toward midnight, when night settled in upon us and María slept like a baby, turned on her right side, her head leaning on her arm, I noticed a few moles that I hadn't seen on her right ear. It seemed that the calm outside had infected her, gotten inside of her and possessed her. I missed seeing her open eyes and I caressed her neck. She looked at me and smiled, still far from this world. I wasn't sure if this was liking the pleasure of my kiss or a half-asleep sensation. I started kissing her again until I ended up on the lobe of her ear, which was cold. A few seconds went by before she answered. She opened one eye slowly, with difficulty, she took my hand and gave it a slow kiss; I felt the wetness of her mouth and leaned close to her side, caressing her hair. Her body, pulsing with life, called to me and I let myself go toward her center like a place I knew well. We lay still while the passion mounted without overwhelming or abandoning us. Our skin opened completely and our hips exploded into heat caused by a shot of intense pleasure, and we let ourselves spill into each other like rivers in the sea.

Outside there wasn't even a gust of wind. Jim brings us coffee and tells us that the danger consists in not being able to arrive at a bay or a cove to shelter ourselves before David comes down on us. The little motor barely keeps going at five miles an hour, because it is only designed to help bring the boat into port. It isn't used for navigation. The radio announces that the hurricane has already reached a velocity of 120 knots per hour and that it will be arriving at the coast of Puerto Rico on the morning of the twenty-ninth. At the rate we're going we definitely won't reach any of the islands to the southeast of the Dominican Republic, where Jim wants to shelter the boat.

2 P.M.

María is at the tiller. I watch her from far away. I see that a very soft breeze manages to lift the tips of her hair, which is hanging loose. Jim shouts, "Here it comes," and he climbs the mast to open the sails for the winds that are coming before the hurricane will bring us close to shore. But he hasn't managed to open all the canvas when we feel a hard shove that seems to come from the hand of God. It's David's first blow. We sail in a northeast direction looking for the Mona Channel, but the force of the wind forces us to go wherever it wants. Jim climbs back up the mast to open the sails a second time because the force of David threatens to turn us over or break the masts. When he comes back, the boom hits him hard. We were close to being without a captain. Still he managed to grab hold of one of the railings at the back of the boat to keep himself from falling into the sea and he hung there until Dodge helped him back up on deck.

We are at the mercy of David's tail because the center is passing some ten miles to the north of where we are. To sail against the wind is impossible, so Jim has decided to let it carry us. We are going at a speed of eighty knots, slicing through the waves as if we were surfing. Jim has replaced María at the tiller and it takes nearly all the strength he has to keep us on course. The wind sounds as if it came from Hell or was moving toward it; the atmosphere is heavy with dust, and it could be said that just one match, if you could light it, would make the Caribbean explode in flames. Everything reeks of salt and iodine.

Several hours go by—I've lost count—sailing at David's whim. The wind has at last gone down a little and Jim takes advantage of it to unfurl the canvas and to straighten the course toward the northeast with an eye toward trying to drive to the Mona, making use of the fact that David must have cleared the channel of the Cuban coastguard. It's a risky maneuver, but there's no other way. I trust María, who hasn't shown the least bit of fear.

10 P.M.

We're entering the channel, cutting across the waves and maintaining our course. Dodge feeds us peanuts. The radio announces that David is shifting toward the coast of Nicaragua, leaving our route free of winds.

The lights of Cuba begin to appear in the distance while the wind is calming down. It's possible that by tomorrow at noon Jim will tell us that we've overcome the danger. The marimba is a little wet and Dodge is worried. Not me, because I saw it being pressed and not even a bullet could get inside those solid masses. The press weighs fifty tons, and it can turn a tungsten diamond into flour. So much so that the mules—the ones on four legs—can only carry two packs on each side, and, even then, they almost can't get down the Sierra.

11 P.M.

Marimba runs from north to south, from Mexico to Colombia and from Colombia to Peru. On the other hand, cocaine travels the opposite direction: from Peru to Colombia and from Colombia to Mexico. María took a little of the herb to Bolivia in order to open a market and find an established team that could bring the coke to Colombia. The connection had been made for her by Robinson, a single-minded gringo whom she spent a long time trying to locate.

The laboratories she was familiar with in Bogotá were small, and as they were also few in number they sold their work for a high price. The large ones had very few cooks and the small ones did their cooking almost in secret. María needed a real wholesaler, and she went out to look for one convinced that she would find him on the very same Seventh Avenue in Bogotá. The key, according to her, consisted in finding a dealer who was free and independent and not getting involved in being one more link in the chain. For that reason, dressed in her always distinctive style—one time elegant like a lady, the next simple like a kid from the La Perseverancia neighborhood—she walked up and down Seventh looking for her man. She had to be very careful because the CIA and the DEA put agents in the field in order to seize the networks. She knew how to distinguish DAS's undercover cops because they were crude; they liked to play at being James Bond, making themselves out to be machos. "And that act," María said, "every woman was wise to it." Her natural instincts helped her avoid the Colombian cops. The gringos were more careful, but they didn't let themselves get familiar because they wanted to get down to business quickly and close the deal without a lot of small talk. María knew how to hold out and wait.

The first days were dedicated to finding out which ones were simply dealers and which ones might be wholesale businessmen. Given this step she had to choose three to be "hers." Everything began with a silent exchange of glances, then an invitation to coffee and later a talk to feel each other out, which, if it ended up in bed, sowed doubts. Her workers asked for it but they didn't give it, and if they did it, it was only in order to float a motive and to study a client up close. She crossed Robinson's path in Parque Santander. They had their first coffee in La Romana and saw each other again the next day. She was gaining confidence in him because he didn't bring up the subject. But one afternoon, after making love in Hotel Santander where Robinson was staying, she asked him if he liked cocaine. He responded disdainfully. A good sign, according to her. They went down that route until he told her that he had a network in Bolivia.

They put things together and María, whom Robinson knew as Azucena, made up her mind to go to Bolivia to talk to the contacts face to face. To flatter them she packed three small packages of the best herb she could find. She glued them into a double bottom and took the plane as far as Pasto. From there she went south on the ground.

She slept in Ipiales and the next day arrived at the border carrying a suitcase with a double bottom. The border guard saw a young, good-looking girl and told her to stand by herself. He told her, "Look, my child, you have to be very careful because the world is a wicked place and you never know who is who or whom you're talking to. They can put marijuana in your suitcase and you'll be going around without even knowing you've got it." Azucena thanked him sincerely for his advice and went on ahead. That same night she arrived in Quito. An outrageous homosexual, wearing pink pants and a yellow shirt, was staying at the hotel. They became friends, and it turned out that he too was heading south, so she decided to let him join her, since everything would be cheaper and sleeping together didn't present any sort of danger. The next day, when they were heading out, they met up with two Argentines who were driving back home. They became friends, and the boys ended up inviting Azucena and the Spaniard to make the trip together with them. The Argentines were on vacation and were rabid fans of the River soccer team. The car was red and white, crammed with banners, flags, coats of arms, and stickers of the team. A car that the whole world looked on as a scandal. She said, "I'll take it."

The Argentine who rode in the passenger seat was drinking and he sang tangos to the driver so that he wouldn't fall asleep. They were rich. The tango singer owned a wine cellar and he had a trunk full of wine in the car that they were drinking and passing around. In one stretch of driving they arrived in Guayaquil and then at the border with Peru, and there, when the police realized that a Colombian was aboard, they began to search the car. Azucena was shaking. But suddenly the captain shouted to the other cops, "Let them go, they're my friends." The Argentines had given him a gift of a bottle of wine.

Then Lima. There they split up. The Argentines went on ahead with the little Spaniard and Azucena checked into the first hotel she found. She slept for the next two days and on the third, ready for the trip to Bolivia, she learned that elections were being held the following Sunday and, for that reason, a coup d'état was a certainty. In Bolivia there are coup d'états for any reason at all, or so they told her. Because they don't like the president, or because the wife of the prime minister is a communist, or because the price of tin fell, or because there are elections, or because there aren't. Azucena unpacked and decided to wait out the coup so that the border would get back to normal. However, two and then three days went by and there was no coup. There were elections and nothing happened; the military stayed put. But everyone insisted that the coup was already on its way and would happen soon. Azucena, without money, alone, eager to hit the road and with the grass in her suitcase.

One hot afternoon she asked if there was ocean near Lima. "Yes," they told her, "It's in Callao." She put on her bathing suit underneath her clothes and went to the beach. She got there really wanting to swim, but she couldn't dive into that gray ocean full of algae and covered with fog. She was tired out when she went back and overheard vallenatos playing in a cevicheria.[7] It was owned by a Colombian who, when he discovered that Azucena was too, suggested she help him work in the restaurant. She was delighted, because at that point she only had the money for the trip from Lima to La Paz.

She worked for a spell and, when everything indicated that the military was getting along with the new government, she decided to book passage on the bus and say good-bye to Lima. Nevertheless, when she arrived at the border she found to her surprise that Generalissimo García Mesa had carried out a coup d'état and the crossing was closed. Nothing to be done about it. She was stuck in a nasty, miserable town named Desaguadero.[8] Three houses on one side of the road and two on the other, all of them residences doubling as hotels where they didn't rent private rooms but rather beds in rooms that held between six and twelve people.

The driver of the bus wanted to go back to Lima, but since all the passengers had bought tickets for La Paz the man, after three days on the border and faced with everyone's loud grumbling, decided to return the fares. There were six foreigners: Azucena, two Uruguayans thrown out of Colombia, a Swiss-German couple, and a Norwegian policeman. The border guard invited the foreigners for a drink of coca tea, which ended with a shot of pisco and then a bottle, and then another, and another.[9] Lieutenant Blanco, as he was known, used this system to investigate those he suspected. In the middle of getting plastered he would get his hands on the information he wanted and, the next day, his friends would wake up his prisoners. Azucena caught the trick and spilled the drinks she was served without being seen. But the lieutenant, as stubborn as he was, started to look only at her and to talk only with her, and she felt certain that she had given everything away. She kept thinking that the lieutenant knew everything until, when everyone else had gone to sleep, she said to him, "Look, lieutenant I'm going to tell you the truth. I'm going to Brazil to finish my studies in religious science and ethics at the Santo Tomás Graduate Institute in Brasilia, and that's all there is to it. I'm not going to sleep with you." The lieutenant, who was a fox, replied: "No, it's true I'm not going to sleep with you. What I want is for you to tell me what you have in your suitcase." She felt that she had been caught but, without giving herself away, she said, "I'll tell you tomorrow."

That night Azucena lay down in her bed to cry, fear on all sides. She woke up crying. At five in the morning she went to the lieutenant's, put the six-pound container on his desk, sat down in front of him, and said while she took a deep breath, "You've got only two choices: either you buy the container from me or you take me prisoner." The lieutenant turned white. He wasn't expecting such defiance. Azucena read the answer in his eyes and offered him a puff; he smoked and took a thousand dollars out of the drawer. He said to her, "I'm not going to steer you off the nice road you're on. But one thing for sure, when you come back this way, I expect to see you wearing a habit."

She went on to La Paz. She stayed in the hotel that Robinson had told her about, she called the guys that she was looking for, and she lay down to wait. A little while later they knocked on the door. She opened and almost passed out: a general in person with three body-guards. "Let me introduce myself, señorita: I am General Ghens, the new government's minister of the interior." Azucena thought that the lieutenant had spilled the beans. But it wasn't so. The general had seen her passing on the street and fallen in love with her. They ate in the best restaurant in town; everything was perfect. When Azucena got back to the hotel, her contacts had left a message saying that because of who she was hanging out with no one could get close to her and that, well, they were sorry, but good-bye, everything was canceled.

Nothing could be done. Robinson was gone, the contacts had rejected her, and she didn't dare to find new ones no matter how many days she hung around, going from bar to bar and side to side. The general continued to dote on her and ended up sending her on a military plane direct to Lima. She returned to Bogotá worn out, with two hundred dollars.

June 28

Today nothing unusual happened: Azucena is more lovely with each passing day. Sargassos in the current: floating islands, fish nurseries.

June 29

Azucena just shouted. She dove into the open sea with Jim because the water looked so mild and seductive. They had swum around the sailboat naked, they had played around until, tired, they started climbing up to the deck on the little wooden staircase. She ahead, he behind, when suddenly a shadow beneath the surface made Azucena shout at Jim, "Watch out, they'll bite you!" No sooner said than done, a hammer-head shark took a lunge at him and missed carrying off his leg by a few inches.

I saw the animal from the prow: it was no less than twenty-three feet from its tail to its eyes, one on both sides of the hammer—tough, fierce eyes that gave me chills. We are now only a day away from the place where we will meet the ship that should come for the marimba.

We just saw a light crossing the horizon. It has an orangy head and a green and bluish body; it was visible for more than thirty seconds and left us open-mouthed. We turned on the radio to see if there was a gigantic meteor or a Russian nuclear bomb dropped on New York. Nothing. Not a single reference to the subject. A total mystery. Our thirst is tightening its grip once more now that there is very little fresh water left.

June 30

The sea lit up like a swimming pool. Around eleven in the morning a pair of dolphins visited us, leaping around the *Rochi*, making their little yelps, not the sound of a bird or a child but saying *thanks, thanks,* bathing in the air, then disappearing. They made love right in front of us, she on the bottom and he on top, squeezing her with his fins and caressing her with his nose. They talk to each other, they coo, they murmur. They touched all of us, and a half hour later no less than a hundred dolphins, an entire country, attach themselves to the boat. They leap out of the water in twos and threes, chase each other, shout or cry; some make love, others caper about, the mothers protect their children and prod them with their noses to jump out of the water. An enormous party that lasts for more than two hours.

Little by little they were disappearing, until the water returned to its monotony, and we to our silence.

July 1

Dodge asks me what I'm going to do with the money. I tell him that what I earned is already collected and safe in Santa Marta. That Jim had paid me to put the marimba on the sailboat and everything after was an adventure for me.

In the afternoon our alarm went off when we saw a gringo battleship far off, crossing toward the west. All night we heard noises and saw strange lights. It calmed me to think that they were thunder and lightning, but when I mentioned this to Jim he said, "Take a good look at what you're seeing!"

July 2

To starboard there are not one but two battleships, and further in an enormous aircraft carrier. There are torpedo boats on all sides and jets are crossing over our heads. "Are they waiting for us?" I asked Jim, who thought my joke extremely dumb. The radio explained that these are naval maneuvers celebrating the fourth of July holiday, Independence Day. There's no danger, but Jim thought it prudent to move away from the area. The problem was that the boat that is going to take the bales from us can't get close, and if the maneuvers go on much longer we could even lose contact.

We sail several miles back to the west. I can see that Azucena is bored. She hasn't gone back to telling me her stories. She's stopped doing things for the *Rochi*, and she hasn't returned to writing nor painting trees with thousands of branches and women with enormous eyes as deep as craters. I think she feels trapped in her own body.

I kill time talking with Dodge, trying to break down the distance that has grown up between us. He has been sailing since he was very young, was an official in Anastasio Somoza's police, and later a gunman for the Baldeblánquez during their war with the Cárdenas. He says that a Kogey wise man cursed both families because Toño Cárdenas and Juanito Baldeblánquez had robbed an Indian woman together, they had raped and then killed her, and thrown her in Rio Ancho. Not only had they killed an indigenous woman but they had deceived a wise man.

Dodge had helped to blow up Toño's fortress house and had fired at the caskets of two of his body guards during the burial.

His stories bored me because they were so pompous and longwinded. But Jim likes him because he knows how to be faithful.

It poured. We were able to collect an abundant supply of drinking water.

July 3, 4, 5

We've waited for three days for the gringo ships to go back to their bases. Everyone on board is drunk except Jim, who stays happy when he's out on the ocean. Jim is a strange man. I've left off his story in the middle of telling it. I'll go back and pick up the thread.

In Guatemala he parted with the circus and went to Medellín, hoping to meet up with Azucena. She was in Bogotá and he found her there, on Seventh Avenue and Jimenez, in the middle of "Operation Robinson," and for that reason she didn't greet him or even look at him. They ran into each other at the house of Conny, a mutual friend, Cuerpo de Paz, who had made a lot of money sending small amounts of cocaine to New York in magazines. Jim was fascinated by the emeralds on Fourteenth Street. He bought an assortment worth ten thousand dollars that turned out to have "clouds," but he quickly learned to recognize purity and he decided to buy stones in Coscuez and Quípama to sell in New York. He transported them in the space between his molars that a skillful dentist had fixed for him. He not only got back the money he had lost but in one year managed to save enough to buy the *Rochi* in the same Taiwanese dockyards, while Azucena traveled to Bolivia with the grass in order to find the network selling the coke that Robinson had sold her. They met up three months later at Conny's in order to make the shipment that all of us were working on. Since she wasn't able to hook up with the Bolivian network, he then insisted on the weed.

July 6
Finally it looks like the last boat has left the area. Jim has been almost crazy for three days trying to communicate with his brother in order to unload the shipment, but it seems to me that he's lost contact.

All night he struggles with the radio. Nothing. Arthur, his brother, does not respond.

July 7,8,9
Nothing at all. Not even a sigh. The food is gone. There's a half-pound of peanuts and raisins left and we're a 120 miles from the coast. If we don't make contact between today and tomorrow we'll be forced to throw the grass overboard. Azucena is opposed, and she argues that it would be better to take the risk of landing at a small dock in order to stock up on provisions and call Arthur on a telephone. The risk is high, but all of us agree that it's the only solution. Hunger has us cornered.

July 10
Jim decides that we'll dock at San Fernandina, and we turn the prow in that direction. We tie up at four in the afternoon. Azucena has put her shoes on and is going with me to buy supplies while Jim calls his brother and Dodge watches the *Rochi*.

Sharon's Diary

I can barely stand up on dry land. I'm seized by a nausea that forces me to sit down for a while. Azucena is still laughing about my dry hangover. I get over it when we walk into the supermarket. We take a cart and fill it up with every kind of meat, pickles, cheeses, fruit, salad greens, wines, and beer. I have the most delicious ice cream I've ever eaten in my life and no matter how long a time it is and no matter what deserts are mine to cross, I won't taste anything like that again. We get back to the boat happy. Jim is too. His brother made contact and he's on course to meet us, toward midday, thirty miles outside where we are. Dodge sets out a banquet and everyone gets drunk. Azucena wakes up at my side.

July 11

Jim yells that his brother is coming in his tugboat. Everyone on board is overjoyed, me in particular. We transfer the crates and separate from Arthur's boat. At four in the afternoon we tie up in Gainesville. Dodge stays behind to take care of the boat while we go into the city, a university town where Jim studied Latin American literature, read García Márquez, and became friends with the poet Álvaro Tenorio. We set about getting drunk again in a student bar, going over the trip, and when we were heading back we see that there's an uproar down by the docks, right next to the *Rochi*. At exactly that moment they lead Dodge out in handcuffs and push him into a patrol car. He catches sight of us but doesn't want to look our way for fear we will be involved in the gravity of the situation. I believe he didn't think we were already involved.

They inform Jim that they have seized the sailboat during a regular inspection. There were marijuana seeds on the floor and, what's more, the walls smelled of grass. The first was a half-proof, the second not. The most serious problem was that Azucena's papers were left behind on the *Rochi* and the police no doubt have them.

July 12

Jim hired a lawyer for Dodge, and Arthur just now gave his brother some 250,000 dollars. We decided to travel to Bloomington, Indiana, where Jim knows people who can hide us in a house in hill country.

August 4

I close the diary here. It's 5:15 in the afternoon. Jim bought an alcoholic's birth certificate for Azucena. From today she'll be known as Sharon, twenty-four years old, wearing her hair very close cut. I don't know where to grab hold of it.

The Nun

Carabanchel August 21, 1993

Most Beloved Mother Superior:

I, Mercedes of Father Damian of Veuster, humble servant of Our Lord Jesus Christ and his slave in the community of Redeemer Sisters, to whom I have delivered my life and taken vows of obedience, poverty, and chastity, throw myself at your feet, crying fresh tears of sorrow, with the hope that in your wisdom and infinite pity you will hear my plea and accept my sincere and profound repentance. I know that I, like any other sister, am unworthy of wearing the habit that I have stained and insulted, that my sin must be purged in prison because I have offended my neighbor, and that only the Highest One knows how much repentance and weeping the crime I committed have cost, and still cost, me. I address you confident that you will accept my words and give credence to them and, that like the sinner I am, you will let me be welcome in your embrace, to find there the forgiveness I seek.

Most Beloved Mother, I will make a detailed account of the calvary that I have lived through since I left your beloved mission in San Antonio, on the banks of the Rio Guaviare, eight months ago now. Eight months in which I have written a letter to your reverence each month explaining my sorrow. Today I want and need to communicate to you each and every suffering that lodges in my heart and, by way of confession, each and every one of the deeds that encroach upon my passion.

I served for more than three straight months in San Antonio, carrying the light of the Gospel to that dark corner, until one day Sister Lourdes informed me that I had received permission to go to live for a time in my hearth and home, where my elderly parents, surrounded by the virtues that grace their age, were anxiously waiting for me. I obeyed, in spite of the fact that it was a terrible burden to leave my jungle and my people, some of them kind and good, and others—just like everyone else—sinners. Even sadder was my parting in which I felt that my work contributed to carrying God's work among men and that in my absence the other sisters would have to replace me and increase their load, heavy in itself.

San Antonio is a small community founded in that region during the time of the war with Peru. Our house sat by the banks of the river and from there you can watch the covered canoes arrive, loaded with catfish that can measure as much as 6 feet long and weigh up to 360 pounds. The Guaviare River is full of those animals, and no matter how long or how much man tracks them down and kills them, the number of fish in the river doesn't decrease. The Indians hunt them, and I don't say fish for them because to kill them is a task where it's harpoons and hooks that win out rather than bait. They are good Indians, clean, who respect God and man in spite of having been as persecuted as the catfish are by other men, ourselves, known as white men, since we deny them recognition as neighbors and at times even of fellow men. In the past they fished for what they needed; they went out from shore in their canoes to watch the forest, catching only a pair of fish or hunting down field rats. They didn't lack for anything; I'd say not even the holy Gospel, because they knew how to listen to the word of God through the murmurs of the jungle and the current of the rivers. Perhaps they didn't know who Jesus was, but they knew how to love their children and their parents. They had their shamans, who didn't teach them the Bible, but they knew how to distinguish between good and evil.

A hundred years or more ago the white man arrived to impose the rubber madness, forcing them upon pain of death to strip the rubber tree. They prohibited them from working as they did before, so that they would have to depend upon the white man, made them feel shame about their naked bodies so that they would have to buy clothes, corrupted them with salt and sugar so that they would go into debt with the store owners, got them drunk on aguardiente and rum so they would leave off drinking chicha.[1] They enslaved them and cut off their ties to the past, their work, their community.

When the rubber fever passed they set them to hunt and kill every animal with fur that moved throughout the jungle. They exchanged the skins for gunpowder, for aguardiente, for salt. One day cocaine arrived in these parts, and from then on they made them harvest it. The Indians were familiar with it and had used it—just as the white man uses coffee—to help them, to keep from being tired, and to speak with their gods. They built laboratories on the banks of the river and everyone devoted themselves to harvesting coca and manufacturing the paste. The businessmen who sold fish started to buy it. They built cold storages in order to freeze the big catfish, which in reality became suitcases stuffed with cocaine. The fish were shipped out frozen with five and even ten kilos of cocaine in their bellies. There were two air companies that shipped the fish. The police took payoffs from one, the army the other. Everyone knew that each shipment of fish was a shipment of cocaine, and that was the way the town lived.

I went back to Bogotá on one of those flights. We left at five in the afternoon and landed at eight at night. The cold was terrible and the airplane practically a refrigerator. As soon as we landed at El Dorado Airport they loaded the fish into some trucks, and they faded away at full speed. That was the way they always did it.

They welcomed me to my house joyfully. I hadn't seen my parents for almost three years, and three years, for old folks, is a long time. They were truly happy to see me and, above all, Mother, that you had given me permission to live with them. My older sister, Amanda, gave me her bedroom; everyone was anxious to take care of me. My father had been a sergeant in the army until they discharged him and he passed the few days of life left to him playing pinochle with his friends, getting on line at the Social Security office to see a doctor, and cashing his pension check at the Agrarian Bank. My mother did everything a mother does: she prayed, cleaned, and organized the house, she sewed but she didn't cook. She had money in the bank and with the interest she paid a maid to prepare the food just the way my father liked it: without salt, cold and simple like in the barracks. All of us learned to eat without enthusiasm, like it was an unpleasant task, because my father ate as if he were going out to fight a war. My mother said that cooking for him turned into a thankless task and that was why she spent her money on a cook.

Amanda worked in a beauty salon. She was a famous hairstylist in the neighborhood. Fridays and Saturdays girls waited on line for her to cut their hair or style it. Although I didn't like the atmosphere of the beauty salon (the gossip among the clients shocked me), I accompanied her there and learned how to give manicures. I thought it would be useful for me to learn to take care of the hands in order to put them to the service of the Eucharist. Padre Eustaquio came from San José the first Sunday of every month to celebrate Mass in San Antonio and we were required to show him healthy and clean hands so as to be able to participate in the sacred service.

Amanda is a beautiful woman, Mother. She has dazzling eyes and thick eyebrows; she's done crazy things in her life and has no desire to get married. She has admirers—many. All of them propose marriage, but she doesn't take them seriously because she says that with obligations come hardships. She introduced one of her most faithful admirers to me, Otto—with two *t*s because he is the son of an Austrian—who she said was a businessman, builder, and exporter. He seemed to me a very serious man, of few words but always attentive. He didn't like drinking, he lived with his son, and seemed very in love with my sister.

One afternoon he invited us to see the Cathedral of Salt in Zipaquirá.[2] I had never seen it and always meant to because Monsignor Augusto Aristizábal, my tutor, had spoken to me about its beauties, considering it to be the eighth wonder. So we went, with Otto and Amanda. In Chía Otto invited us to eat yucca bread and in Cajicá we stopped to look at some small throw rugs made from virgin wool that he wanted to make a deal for so he could send them to other countries, where they got a good price. While we were eating lunch at the Liberator Inn, he asked me questions about my life in the community, about my work and what I needed. I told him everything because he seemed to me a very respectable gentleman, although Amanda didn't take him seriously.

A week later he showed up at the beauty salon. He waited for us while we finished our jobs and then offered to drive us home in his car. On the way he asked me, without any evil intent, if I knew anything about Spain. I told him I had never been out of the country because there were many outposts here but that our main parish was in Valladolid. I told him that the community also had missions among the blacks in Africa and that what I wanted one day was to become a servant on that continent. Father Damian was the role model for my life, so much so that my convent name, Mother mine, as you may recall is Mercedes of Father Damian of Veuster.

Sister, he said to me, I have a trip next week to Madrid. I am going to take samples of typical woolen throw rugs, but the trip is giving me trouble because my sister is coming from Argentina at the same time to visit me. Couldn't you help me out? All you have to do is carry the samples for me and you're done. I will pay for your journey, with about two thousand dollars more for your expenses and to compensate for any trouble.

I didn't tell him yes or no. But I dreamed about the trip because perhaps being in Spain I could ask to be transferred to the headquarters in Valladolid and from there jump to Africa.

Most Serene Mother: I beg you to consider, in your holy wisdom, the purity of my decision. For more than eight days I prayed steadfastly to the sacred hearts of Jesus and Mary to enlighten me and fill my soul with Saint Teresa's prayer:

> Sweet life, sun without curtains
> I keep myself apart from all of it —
> What do you have in mind for me?

God chooses you treacherously and sends you the cross with the most unknown emissaries. You know my soul and how much love there is within for service, although my talents are scant and my light small. I answered Otto that, fine, I would do the favor for him with great pleasure. Amanda thanked me and everyone in the house was happy, because it was an honor for all of us that a member of the family would have the opportunity to see another country.

Otto explained the particulars of the trip to me: at Barajas, the Madrid airport, a man named Samuel would approach me as soon as I got off the plane; he would greet me; I would give him the suitcase with the samples, and he would take me where I asked and we would be done. Assignment completed. Otto would give me the two thousand dollars in advance.

My error, Mother, which I could never amend and will never wash away, although you can see all the tears that I am still crying, was in not having consulted with the religious community, and especially with you, about the decision that I took. Perhaps the devil, who always appears to us as vanity, took the words out of my mouth and counseled me not to consult with Your Reverence in Colombia but rather to announce from Spain my decision to serve in Africa. I wanted to give you a surprise so that I couldn't retreat. I made this decision in secret and I recognize that my aspiration was full of pride. This is the sin that I have to purge, carrying the cross that I bear now.

I asked Otto how Samuel would know that I was the one that he was looking for, and he said to me that it was very easy. I would go dressed like all nuns when they travel: long black skirt, white blouse, black sweater. He had studied me closely, and I didn't have to say more than yes to everything. Everything fit together so well that I had no reason to suspect anything. Maybe on the day of the trip I felt a doubt, like a shadow, as to whether I would really be carrying rug samples. But I immediately rejected my distrust like an evil prejudice toward a fellow man about whom I had no right to suspect anything evil because he hadn't done anything bad to me.

The morning of the trip Otto arrived bright and early at the house with two suitcases. I had thought there was only one. Two huge suitcases that he opened in front of everyone, letting me see the samples of the rugs. All of them were exactly the size of the suitcase. He told me that, obviously, he would pay for the excess baggage. He gave me eighteen hundred dollars and five thousand pesetas for tips and taxis and so I wouldn't have to go looking for a Money Exchange,[3] as tired as I was going to be when I arrived at Barajas.

I said good-bye to my adored father with so much love, thinking as I then thought that I would be leaving for Africa and, although no one knew that, my farewell could be the last. I asked for his blessing on my knees, I listened lovingly to his advice, and then said good-bye to each and every one of my family members because I knew that my absence was going to be a long one. I began to feel the arrogance of what one can get away with and, what's more, of what is admirable, and I wept for my weakness and susceptibility.

I didn't have any major problems in the airport. The plane scared me on account of its being such a long flight, but I consoled myself thinking that my God has a goal in mind and that against his power nothing is possible except submission. The flight made a stop in Santo Domingo, where we had to wait more than six hours. Something had gone wrong on the plane because when we took off it sounded as if we were being torn apart from the inside. I prayed in the airport chapel for all my fellow men and I begged Father Damian to intercede with his light so that my superiors would accept my desire to serve in Africa. Having served in my country, in Puerto Mastranto, in the Llanos Orientales, in El Palmar in the Sierra Nevada, in San Benito near the equator, and in Poparandó, in northeast Antioquia, I had covered the cardinal points of Colombia and I wanted to find, Mother mine, a Molokai where I could do as Father Damian had done: "I became a leper among the lepers, and if I can't cure them at least I can console them."[4]

We arrived in Madrid the next day. I had lost count of the hour because I had watched the dawn and nightfall several times. I was groggy when I descended from the plane. Dazed by so much sleeplessness, I arrived at customs and showed them my papers.

They asked me why I had come; I told them I came to spend my vacation. The official didn't find anything irregular. He closed the passport and told me, "Have a nice vacation, sister. You may go."

I picked up my suitcases and began to feel strange that Mr. Samuel hadn't come up to greet me. In my excitement I hadn't even thought to ask what Samuel looked like. I moved to the side so I wouldn't be in the way. Everyone looked to me like Samuel. But no. Nothing. No one came up to me. I hadn't even thought of this possibility. I thought about calling Bogotá on the telephone, but I was afraid because I didn't know how to do it. I waited for an hour and then said to myself, "OK, since the plane has landed and the man hasn't arrived, I'll go to a hotel and call Bogotá." I hailed a taxi, asked the driver if he could take me to a decent, cheap hotel, and as the cab was coming to a stop I noticed a policeman running up to the side.

"Stop where you are!" He ordered.

I thought that I had forgotten something on the sidewalk, but no. The policeman came right up to me and said, "Did they check your bags, Your Reverence?"

"Yes," I told him, "Everything is in order."

"Would you please come with me?"

"Of course," I said. I got out. I was surrounded by police. A fat man, with half a head of hair left, spoke to me.

"You are a nun, is that right?"

"Yes, that's right, sir, I am a sister in the Congregation of the Redeemer Sisters."

"Pleased to meet you," he said. "I am Samuel. You almost got away from us with the contraband, didn't you?"

"Contraband?" I asked. "You're confusing me. What is this? Of course I brought the rug samples that Mr. Otto sent for you."

"Ah ha. Very good, very ingenious. Let's take a look at the sample that our friend Otto sent for us."

They opened the suitcases and went through my things. I blushed when I saw the police looking at them, examining and sniffing every one of my private items. I said to Mr. Samuel, "You know who I am. Please, explain to them who I am. Gentlemen, don't treat me this way. What is this? What's it about? What are you looking for?"

One of them found my habit, took it out, unfolded it, and held it out in front of the others.

"Here it is, this is who we've been waiting for: the little nun. Your Reverence, what do you have in your suitcases?"

"Rugs," I said.

"Rugs? Let's take a look. Let's look at the rugs," said Mr. Samuel, and they started to take them out.

I remained calm, although I was becoming more disturbed with each passing moment. The rugs were sewn together and between one and another, also sewn into place, was a large, thin plastic bag with many flat compartments. Everyone was watching me. I couldn't bring myself to admit what there was stored in those tiny and neatly packed baggies. The police laughed and looked at me. They were putting the powder together and placing it on a scale. A scale, beloved Mother, just like the one they use in San Antonio to weigh the cocaine. So then I realized that what I had brought was cocaine, pure cocaine. That was the contraband which they were scoffing about. I couldn't say that I hadn't brought what I had brought.

The police doctor told me, "That will get you, sister, between sixteen and twenty-five years, depending on whether you go along with them."

An officer in front of me counted out the eighteen hundred dollars and the five thousand pesetas. Another guard came close to me, asked me to hold my arms out and put on the handcuffs. I collapsed in sobs. They carried me to an office where they recorded my data and put me through a more than two-hour interrogation. What I didn't know, Mother of mine, was that they were writing my dossier and that you never choose the cross you have to carry because if it were like that it wouldn't be a cross.

They carried me out in handcuffs, dragging my clothes suitcase as well as I could; the others, where the rugs or contraband were stored, stayed behind as part of the dossier. At one in the morning I entered what I later knew was called Plaza de Castilla. They put me in a cell alone. A doctor came by, and the jailhouse lawyer who advised me to deny everything, that it wasn't fair, that I couldn't pay for what others had done, and then they let me make a phone call. My sister Amanda began to scream and yell how was it possible that I was involved in such a crime, she was going to kill Otto, she was going to tear out his eyes. She couldn't, because Otto never came back to let her get a good look at him.

Nor could I say anything substantial about Otto because—the truth will out—I didn't know anything different from what I had said and that wasn't enough for him to be arrested by the authorities as an accessory. But I couldn't lie. I said to Samuel, Mr. Samuel, while looking into his eyes, "Why do you do things like this? Why do you make others suffer? Why do you want to make your living in such a wretched way? Can you feel affection for your children with such a dirty heart?"

He slapped me. I didn't turn my face to let him hit the other cheek because I was angry, Mother, and I forgot that Christ had buried "an eye for an eye" in order to give birth to "the other cheek."

Later they carried me off to a cell where there were gypsies shouting and pulling out their hair in clumps. They had been caught selling heroin, which in Spain they call horse. They had "the monkey," an attack of nerves you get when you consume drugs.[5] They were like madwomen. They vomited and groaned. Only one, whose name was Victoria, cried by herself in a corner without making an uproar. They looked at me as if I wasn't there, but they stared at the suitcase I dragged in. A moment later, one of them named Feliciana came right up to me and yelled, "Everything in the bag is ours. Give up whatever you're carrying because that's ours too."

They threw everything on the ground and were taking everything apart, piling one thing on top of another. Victoria kept crying in her spot without joining the party, and Feliciana grabbed me by the hair, ordered me to strip and put on my habit. I obeyed because I was afraid they would do something to me, and when I had taken off my clothes, all of them, even Victoria, broke out in laughter. So much ballyhoo got the attention of the guard, who came up close to look through the peephole, and a little while later the prison director sent me the penitentiary uniform, a green suit and black shoes. I felt like I was getting out of purgatory.

The judge condemned me, without any protest on my part, to eight years, three months, and a day. The only proof that existed against me was having carried a suitcase with cocaine. Of the 2 kilos that had appeared in the airport, 328 grams were missing, which were split between Samuel, the guards, and who knows who else. They accused me of being a member of the San Jacinto cartel. I didn't understand the accusation, but later I came to understand that it was a matter of a chain of Colombian narcotraffickers who brought drugs to Spain. From time to time those criminals send a marked man. The guards, the investigators, and the antinarcotic brigades—all of whom have business with the major drug dealers in Colombia—arrange things so that someone is caught and they can thereby conceal their collaboration with the Mafia. I left Bogotá marked and they grabbed me, Mother, a religious woman, because in doing so they showed what sharp investigators they are: even a nun falls into their hands. I learned this a little while ago, because in prison everything is out in the open. Everything. A prison is as open inward as it is closed outward. Here, Mother mine, nothing can be hidden. ▓

As you know, I saw the light of day in Abriaquí, a town I never got to know because shortly after I was born they transferred my father to Frontino, where I was raised and grew up. So I am, as I like to think of it, from the same race of Antioquians as the most eminent Mother Laura Montoya, founder of the Order of Lauritas. Frontino is a town, tormented by the civil war, where everyone is a miner, was a miner, or wants to be a miner but where no one has ever become rich being a miner. I finished my bachelor's degree at the Presentation Academy and wanted to study to be a teacher, when one fine day at about four in the afternoon, climbing the main road on foot by myself, as I was looking around at the afternoon I suddenly felt the call of the Holy Spirit: the host of souls, consolation in one's tears, calm shade in the unwavering heat, who with his light illuminated my senses. A large cloud covered the sun, but it let great rays of light cross the heavens. I heard heavy thunder and said, "Lord, I will follow you to the end of my days." Frontino's parish priest, who was a friend of Monsignor August Aristizábal, at that time dean of the Cathedral in Medellín, gave me a letter for him after learning of my decision and the way that the calling manifested for me. The monsignor gave me courage, he asked me to reflect and be modest, but he said that if in three months I persisted in searching for the road of sacrifice, he would help me. He counseled me to read the lives of the saints and gave me Padre Damian's biography.

Three months later there was no doubt. My faith had been fortified and there was no possibility of going back on my decision. I wanted to be a missionary, wanted to place my life at the service of the propagation of the Gospel. The obstacle was that since my father was an honest representative of the law, he had no way of getting the necessary funds. When I said as much to the monsignor, he calmed me down.

"Daughter, God will provide for what is needed. Your willingness is the true gold."

So that was the reason, Mother, that one day I knocked on the door of the Redeemer Sisters in Medellín. I was a runaway from my home, no doubt, but in obeying God's summons I began my religious life right there. I wrote to my parents to tell them what was happening and in six months I was a postulant for admission to the order in Popayán. I learned how to maintain the vow of silence. It was difficult. A person lives in a world full of voices, voices that shout and some that give orders; voices that praise and some that threaten; our own voices and sometimes not our own. If silence doesn't prevail on the outside, it will never take root on the inside. Sister Elena taught me that. It was a time that I cherish and that here in Carabanchel has given me the fortitude necessary not to grow weak and to make my captivity into missionary work. In Medellín, after my novitiate, I was taken on as a young candidate.

I still remember that sunny morning when we put on the habit. There were fourteen steps up to the altar: we novices stayed sitting on the ground for thirty three minutes with crowns of thorns on our heads and our feet on a bed of roses, accepting that suffering is purified by fire. Once the bell had finished sounding twenty five times, announcing to the world that we would live in it without belonging to it, that we were dead to man's vanities and born for the glory of God, I heard the heavenly choirs chanting Hosanna, and when they placed the chasuble on my shoulders I felt all the happiness of being a slave to Christ.

We were assigned to Mutatá. I have been familiar with it since I was a child because it is, along with Dabeiba, the other large town in northwest Antioquia. I only stayed there a few days, the time necessary to prepare, with Sister Martha, the foundation of the mission in Po-parandó, a river whose waters flow into the Atrato. We were going to do what a missionary does: to start a safe haven for the light of the Gospel. We did it just as they ordered us to and, as you know, such as is customary in our order: starting from nothing. Sister Betsabé, who knew the region like no one else, had instructed us thoroughly about how to get there, where to go, and whom to ask for help.

Poparandó is the name of an area in the jungle that forms part of the Embera tribe reservation. We landed on a large beach close to several shacks inhabited by Negroes. When we arrived with Sister Martha they were singing hymns for a baby who had died the night before. The parents, accompanied by the whole community, keep watch over their dead children for the entire night. They pray, sing, and drink rum. The songs for the children who have just died are very beautiful. They come from deep inside. All of them say that the departed one will become a tiny angel and they give thanks to God for having saved the child from the slavery of this world. The Negroes have tremendous faith, which you can hear in the sad songs that always recall their past. It mustn't be forgotten that we white people carried them off by force from their world, which, as I understand it, is very similar to our jungles; we put them to work in the mines at the tip of the lash— work unknown to them—and we forbade them to speak their lan-guage, have their own laws, or support their families. We owe them a great debt that we can probably never pay. The Redeemer Sisters, as you well know, believe the roads leading to God are infinite, and we have no reason to impose one or the other, since the sin of arrogance is not only personal but also collective, belonging to a group, a reli-gious community, or a country.

As soon as we set our feet on the ground, like the Redeemers we are, we set to making a house, building a small room where we could sleep and start our missionary work. Cutting a tree trunk isn't easy; to cut many of them is hard, and to hollow them so that one will fit inside the other and they can be lashed together is almost impossible for people accustomed to giving the things most necessary for survival to others to do. It's the same, Mother, if you ask me, with rice. No one knows the amount of work behind one plate of rice: to clear and clean up a plot by the side of the river, buy the seeds, get the ground ready, pray to San Isidro that it rains on time, not too much nor too little, scare away the birds so that they don't eat the seeds, gather the stalks, ask San Lorenzo to help separate the grain from the chaff, then pound and beat the grain so that it falls loose from the shell, and, finally, to go for wood, to make a fire and not let it get smoky. Each thing that we did to survive was a lesson in suffering, an opportunity to look at our inconstancy, a means to build our new life and to put ourselves at the service of the Negroes and Indians.

Our work in Poparandó was growing little by little. The community was paving the way for us, even so far as to make us part of it. We shared the same needs; they helped us keep our resolve with material things while we helped them find spiritual things on the road of faith and hope. We lived with them for two years, Mother, and we left having created a work that can't properly be called a church but rather the start of a connection. With the young men in the guerrilla army, who at times walked right by the missionary house—a hut with a cross and an azalea bush brought from Medellín—we talked about what for both of us is a surrender to the cause, call it God, your neighbor, or the revolution. The hardship and sacrifice are the same for me and for the other, and our faith, even though put in different forces, is the same.

We made the same connection in Puerto Mastranto, Aruaca, where we were transferred. There, as you will remember, we got to know each other, since you were in charge of the work and the principal at the boarding school. You will remember my effort and my eagerness to make myself more useful to our mission with the Sáliba Indians, with the settlers and the sheepherders. I remember the afternoon that, while we were doing the manual labor you recommended to us, the young guerrilla fighters seized the town. Despite our protests and our outrage, our house and above all the chapel were used as fortifications for shooting at the police. We already knew them and, although we didn't care for the weapons they were carrying, we weren't afraid of them. Just the same, in Puerto Mastranto we saw them fire the guns; we felt the full force of destruction that they possess, and we saw how they were finishing off the police station, forcing the officers to surrender, condemning the sergeant in loud voices and tying him up. All the sisters were weeping, and we begged the comandante not to kill him, saying that this would be an assassination and the revolution ought to be above all Christian and know how to forgive, but we weren't able to move their hearts. They killed the sergeant and we buried him, weeping for him without tears because we had already cried all we had.

From Puerto Mastranto I went to San Benito, a town that, although it is located in Ecuador, is Colombian. Our people go there, above all the Tuquerres, Cumbal, and Guachucal Indians, and those from the Tumaco, Patía, and Guachicono regions, to work on the palm plantations, in the cotton and sorghum fields, in the mines. It's a hot town, full of movement and vice. There are prostitutes and thieves, cantinas and bars, traffic in contraband and streets full of disturbances. Nobody obeys the police or pays attention to the priest. For us to undertake our work in a world mad for money is a great challenge. To make ourselves felt, to put ourselves in the center was almost impossible. No one gave us a hand because everyone was busy doing what they had to do to send a few pesos to their families in Colombia. It fell to us to work in silence, without anyone paying attention and without the hope of being heard. Most difficult of all was having to go to the garbage to sift for remains of food, because no one gave us alms so we could survive. The shopkeepers threw us out of their stores at the top of their lungs; the police watched us day and night, all because we had discovered that the two together had killed an Indian woman. Many days we were very much on our own because the Colombian authorities didn't want to get involved in the case and the Ecuadorians took our testimony as an attack on their country. The murder of laborers and dayworkers is a story that gets repeated over and over in San Benito without anyone denouncing it. We suffered a lot, and that is why I relaxed when they transferred me to El Palmar, in the Sierra Nevada, where I recuperated from my various illnesses.

For a few days at least, because evil was also planting its seeds there, which went by the name of marimba. The Pérez brothers were in charge of it. They were from Tolimen, first cousins of Teófilo Rojas, who became well known as Sparks. They had come there fleeing from the civil war.⁶ They had started their business and made a success of it, become rich and well known. When marijuana came on the scene, they had branched out into it and they stayed rich and famous. It wasn't difficult for them to give the farmers seeds to grow and to fill up bags with the grass they bought in El Palmar and sold in Ciénaga. As they knew how to fire guns, it also wasn't hard for them to get respect from the people living along the coast who bought it and shipped it outside the country, and since guns attract other guns, neither was it difficult to make friends with the captain of the army whose base was in town and to kill the harvesters so as not to have to pay them. El Palmar, La Tebaida, and Año Entrante harvested the dead. Later, when marijuana was over, the guerrillas arrived. The Perez brothers, rich in houses, in businesses, and estates, organized one of the first paramilitary groups in the Sierra Nevada. The dead kept on piling up by the dozens. The suffering of the campesinos was great and our work difficult amid so much bloodshed. I felt terrible sadness when the directorate asked me to go to work in San Antonio, because in El Palmar I wasn't even able to plant a single seed of hope.

I like writing down my memories, Mother, because they make my country live for me once again; because, in spite of the blood and the sadness, the sun is still coming up there and the people keep on outwitting their misfortunes. The people live, and that's why they kill them. And the more they kill, the more your life recovers strength and meaning. Every time Colombians arrive here—and they arrive all the time—I hang around them so that they will tell me what's going on back at home, because they carry their country on their backs.

When I walked in to this place, which suffering transforms into a holy place, I thought that I would go crazy and that everything I had lived was a lie. Nevertheless, I pulled along a string that connected me with my people; I brought, still fresh, the feelings of the last night with my family; the serious face of my father, saying good-bye to me with great feeling in his eyes, certain that he wouldn't see me again; the kiss from my sainted mother, always suffering, always supporting all her children, always concerned about what happens to us; the spirit of my sister, who saw in my trip something like an agreement between her and Otto. But, what's more, I brought nailed to my soul the strength with which the jungle in the Guaviare grows, the clearness of the air in the Sierra Nevada, the cries of the Negro children, the easy familiarity of the Cumbal Indians, the cold on the airplane that carried the fish and the cocaine from San Antonio, the same cocaine the mules carried to Madrid in their intestines or in their suitcases. I arrived here with all of that life, and here it turned into melancholy.

I won't forget, Mother, the moment in which I walked through the doors of Carabanchel, one after the other. They opened up as if they were swallowing me and closed making a harsh noise that resounded in the waiting area like the ringing of the bells in a Mass for the dead. Neither will I forget my encounter with the chabarro, as they call the cell here in Spain, where I would have to remain for eight years: a cubicle twenty-two square feet in size, where two women lived, separated from our families and forgotten by our people. Her name is Monica; she's forty-five years old and has served about forty months behind bars. From Bogotá, married with three children. She took me into her care from the moment I walked in. She introduced me to the others and told me the small secrets one has to know to survive.

"In here you aren't a nun, you're a woman from Colombia who has to respect herself as such. In here we Colombians are a crew that defends itself on all four sides, back pressed against back. The four sides are, first, the prison guards, who are always looking for a way to fuck you over and seize on the negative actions, every one of which will get you three months more behind bars. The guards hate us because we don't bow down to them. The second side are Spaniards who, being that they are on their turf, think we are the Indians that Christopher Columbus discovered, and they treat us like dangerous guests. The third side are the gypsies. Watch out for them because they don't acknowledge or respect anybody: for them the *collai*, those who aren't gypsies, are their enemies. They run the horse, or heroin, trade.

The fourth side are the blacks. They're violent and they're strong and they run the hashish market. With all of them, including the guards, you have to make them respect you: no making jokes, no lowering your eyes, no making deals. Here the deals you have to make you make with your sisters or with nobody. We control the workplaces that give you a chance to serve your sentence more rapidly; we're in charge of the garbage in this area, the cleanliness and hygiene of the common areas, the cabinetmaking and dressmaking workshops, the bakery and the laundromat. We are women who've worked all our lives, and if we are here it's because we took a wrong turn and not because we're evil and corrupt, like the Spanish. Many of us have taken courses here in Spain in the correspondence schools of the University of Education, at the National Institute of Higher Education and the National Educational Center. We've got Colombian graduates here in law and Spanish literature; plenty of women have got their undergraduate degrees; some even have learned how to read and write, and we even have those who don't let their families know they're prisoners but keep up the ruse they're here studying and later arrive in Colombia with their degrees. We Colombian women are the most beaten up, and they put us in the worst positions, in spite of which they live trying to find our weak spot. Because for the people in here cocaine and Colombia are one and the same."

Monica is a heavyset woman, full of strength, who doesn't know how to pray with her lips but only with her arms. She is our center. We cry on her shoulder and we answer to her; she consoles us and defends us. It's said that she loved her man very much, until, as time went by and alcohol was getting the better of him, he gave in, and then she woke up and took charge of the house, of the kids and the debts. But the debts were winning the race and the lawyers were going to throw her out of the house. She said: "No, I'll save it," and she agreed to make a run. You could earn five thousand dollars carrying the cocaine and she, with obligations and threatened with having to live in the street, decided to accept the offer and come loaded down in a large group.

She came like all the rest. For the narcotraffickers we're mere suit-cases, just like the catfish in the Guaviare. They use us as walking baggage and abandon us if we fall, no matter that they promised us every kind of guarantee and assistance. I have come to accept that I was used, that I am therefore one mule more, but, saying that, I don't see myself as having been given to carrying cocaine consciously and voluntarily. I was tricked, like so many, and I have come to accept that I am a mule because I have to pay for my sin like all the other women here, without letting myself be tempted by the vanity of being a reli-gious person and for that reason superior or different from the others. The Redeemers ought to be people who suffer like everyone else and not from the heights of a religious life, looking at the others from atop a pedestal. The only way to know how to help the flock is to be a sheep, and not just a curly white sheep but a black goat, a billy goat, and even a wolf.

And so, because she had no choice, Monica decided to board the plane carrying drugs. She told her children that she was going to buy items for resale. She hadn't gotten onboard when another passenger that she didn't know began to make noise because of air sickness. The stewardesses, who are experts in catching the bad ones, gave her hot milk, which they say breaks the containers; the young girl began to cry desperately and gave one shout after another. She walked on in a panic. The whole plane knew what was going on. A stewardess advised her to pass the bags so that she wouldn't die, and the distraught young woman ran down the aisle to the bathroom and from the aisle to the cabin asking for help. Another young woman was so overwhelmed that she confessed that she too was carrying and she went into a panic that spread to everyone, or nearly everyone. The plane became a house full of madwomen. It seized the whole group, including Monica, who, like everyone else, started to sweat. Then they got chills, until they ended up turning themselves in. It was an Iberia plane and therefore Spanish. So that in Santo Domingo, under the care of the police, the women were taken to the hospital, lifted in the air in order to get the bags out. and, after cleaning out their stomachs, sent back onto the same plane as prisoners, which had to wait for six hours while the mules recuperated. There were nine young women and all of them arrived in Spain with the bags in their hands.

My first days, Mother, were hard days, long and dark because it was wintertime. I was very proper and I reproached myself all the blessed day, blamed myself and accused myself until I realized that loading myself down with guilt was a way of not accepting the weight of the cross. The moment I caught on to my own trick was miraculous. It happened on the birthday of the Infanta, the daughter of the king, which in the Spanish prisons they celebrate by serving beer with the meals. When they handed me mine, a gypsy snatched the glass and tried to drink it. I put my things down and pushed her. She hit me with her fist once and then twice, knocked me to the ground and started kicking me until the guard came up and pushed me out of the dining room violently. They carried me off to the punishment cell and gave me three days of lockup. To her, being from the same country as the guards, they did nothing. So that I came out resentful and armed with courage and a little later I crossed paths with the gypsy in the hallway. I looked at her, I came close to her without being afraid, bent her arm and dragged her off by force to the showers, where I showed her who I was. She spent three days in the infirmary. I am not strong, Mother, but I had to try it and, fighting like all the other women, accept the rules of the game of life behind bars. From that day on the other prisoners call me "Not Coming Back." No one knows who gave me this name, or even less why.

Feeling that I was part of the penitentiary and of the condemned, I found shelter. They offered me a workplace that touched my soul from the first day: working in the gypsies' kindergarten. They are like one big family; they don't separate nor do they let themselves be separated. When one gets sick, they all go to the hospital and the hospital fills up; when one becomes a prisoner and they take him to Caraban-chel, the others pitch camp on a hill by the side of the prison from which they can watch the top floor of the building, and from there they shout lamentations that are like extended cries. The prisoner answers them, and they pass the whole day like that. They don't give up, and they aren't alone in the prison, even if they stay twenty years.

There are always gypsies on the hill, keeping company with those who have lost their liberty. It is very sad, Mother, but at the same time very beautiful.

Victoria, the gypsy who stayed in her corner crying the day that I arrived (when they stole my clothing), is someone whose husband hasn't left her for even one day. He arrives early each morning and begins to weep his troubles and shout his love to her. She answers him in the same way. One shouts, or more accurately sings, and the other answers. At times the voices meet and form a duo that breaks your heart. At times they fight, at times they reproach each other, and I believe that they even piss each other off. One can't understand their words, because they speak "calé," but one can feel them.

Victoria was caught selling horse. Her husband Manuel had been her boyfriend since she was five years old. They lived in Sevilla and from when they were children they were chosen by the elders of both families to be man and wife. They played together knowing that some day they had to tie the knot, and, when at last the marrying age arrived, the adult women got together and discussed with the old folks whether the time for Victoria to let "the drop that flowers fall" had now arrived. They said yes—Manuel was fifteen years old and she fourteen—and the fiesta was arranged. The father of the husband paid the dowry for the bride, which in this case was a late model car—in place of the Andalusian horse, as they used to do—and the day of the celebration arrived. The party started early, and it lasted until late, until the women made a signal to the young people that they should wait in the street and to the rest of the family to leave the newlyweds alone. Victoria and Manuel went to the bedroom. Everyone waited for her to come out to the balcony to show off the sheet stained with the drop of blood, but when they didn't do it the young people left off their jokes and starting sharpening their knives. Time went by and Victoria did not appear, until Manuel's brothers unsheathed their knives and went off to Victoria's father to make him pay in blood for the blood that hadn't stained the sheet.

Ashamed, Manuel and Victoria fled. No one saw them take off, in spite of being watched closely. They went to Jaen and they lived there, hating themselves. Until the day Manuel bought a sex magazine so he could learn what a woman's body was like, to know if something was hidden beneath the brassiere. Time went by and they went back to Sevilla. No one had anything to do with them, no one even said hello. They had been thrown out of the tribe, but one afternoon the oldest woman came out on the balcony shouting and waving the sheet with the drop forming a large flower, already dry, but so large and bright that it seemed alive. The tribe was coming together bit by bit. They embraced the couple, and kissed them; the musicians arrived, the old folks, and, after three months, the party that had been called off was resumed. The couple came out to dance the happiness of weeping, which is the true dance of the gypsies.

Mother, my work with the gypsy children was taking hold of me so much that I put aside my cross, and I requested that they let me work in the hospital, taking care of those dying of AIDS. Father Damian's example with the lepers shows me the way, and that is why I will dedicate myself to being with those poor condemned ones until my last day in prison, making them feel that they are human beings who are dying and not pieces of living junk. To be with those who are passing away in their supreme hour is a final act of love, because death is the only experience of life that isn't shared. My presence at the death of others is my way of not forgetting my cross, of not feeling that I am a solitary condemned person.

Mother mine, at your feet I beg you to read this letter to the Bogotá Mission the next time they meet. Your understanding is forgiveness and forgiveness is a new birth for me. I atone here not only for my sin but also for the sin of my own, of my people. In bearing my cross I help my people carry that which they have put on their shoulders.

Waiting in resignation,
Mercedes of Father Damian of Veuster
Redeemer Sister and servant of
Our Lord Jesus Christ

Puppet

I arrived in Leticia a complete success. I wanted to leave everything that I had been and done behind, in a trunk, and once again plunge into life. I had to drive away the fear that was piling up higher and higher, alongside the big river, while I watched it pass by.

When I was a child watching the waters of the Cauca in La Virginia, where I was born and brought up among women—they had killed all the men one by one—I had a hard time breathing. The women watched over me like a sin. They didn't let me leave the house or see anyone. They played their games with me and not mine. They dressed me as a sailor, they gave me juice with lemon twists and linseed, they changed my name. I liked to look at the photographs that hung in the drawing room, that were only of men. All of them had died and all of them had beards. Those in the fuzziest photographs had died in the wars of a Thousand Days, which my grandmother called the great ones, and had a black sash hung on the corners; the others who had left and never returned had a green sash; and the rest, and there were many, had been killed in the civil war and had a red sash. My grandmother, after praying and weeping, opened the drawing room for me and went along with me to look at the portraits. At times she said to me, "He died in Enciso fighting against General Reyes; this other one died on the plains of Garrapata fighting against General Marceliano Vélez." Of those who returned, she said, "This one had large eyes; that one thick lips," and those who had the red sash she didn't mention. We left in silence. She locked the drawing room with a key and I went to look at the horses. Three sorrels that nobody rode but that had to be put through their paces every day and brushed on Saturdays. I liked to help by throwing water on them and combing their tails.

I had three aunts: Lucila, Graciela, and Dora. They were young and I thought they were pretty, especially Dora, who had green eyes and cold hands. Every night I slept in one of their beds and on Sunday they raffled me off. Lucila liked it when I kissed her shoulders, Graciela when I sang her a ranchera she had taught me, and Dora when I warmed her feet. At nighttime they were all kisses, but during the day they gave me jobs to do and I ended up weeping by the banks of the Cauca. ▨

I had arrived in Leticia from New York, where I had worked the "Don't say a word," a move that Angelino Becara, from Marsella, Caldas had taught me and that consisted in putting the barrel of the gun in the victim's belly and saying, "Don't say a word, you son of a bitch!" I had won his confidence in Ibagué and Pereira, and it was he who helped me go to New York. I sold the gun, left with the money, and packed my bag. I arrived with 500 dollars and the desire to work where I didn't have to put up with being in a plane. I had only one contact: a Colombian who lived in Brooklyn named Amadeo. A serious scoundrel who took 450 dollars from me for a Falcon .357 pistol without saying a word. A pistol six and a half inches long, with twelve shots: the keys to the city.

He set me to getting familiar with the area, my work being to keep an eye on his movement: what the people did, how they moved about, what they took with them, where they were headed. Casing the joint. I went into restaurants, to bars, looking around, moving like a cat, until in one bar I heard a Colombian speaking English. No doubt about it, it had to be a guy from Colombia. I turned around and there the dude was, blabbing away in that English that you can understand in Spanish. He was from Angelópolis. He took me into his confidence and only a short while later gave me various assignments: the Israelis who knew how to carry the diamonds out of the stores under their nails and the rabbis who carried the money to buy the stolen diamonds in their leather briefcases. There was no way to lose: either they were carrying bills or diamonds. They were easy to pick out because they wore black hats, curly sideburns, and large overcoats, also black. Easy targets. The game consisted in following close behind them until one of them passed by a telephone booth and then, "Don't say a word, you son of a bitch!" You pushed the man into the booth with the Falcon, he dropped the briefcase and you kept pointing it at him until he took off. Not one came up empty: five thousand, six thousand dollars or diamonds, gold. I worked between 40th and 55th Streets, between five and six in the afternoon; the rest of the night I drank, had a wild time, and went shopping.

I got to know another Colombian called Tuco, born in El Águila, north of Valle, the very town where my father died. We became friends. He knew a lot. He had put the drop on Sophia Loren for sixty thousand dollars in the Plaza Hotel. He went right up to her room, told her, "Hands up," and the woman gave him what she had with the provision that he not touch her or her son. Tuco, who was very bold, slipped in like the lady's hairdresser and then out, with the job done. He worked alone because he didn't trust anyone, but in order to pull off the job that he had in his sights he needed help: he wanted to hit a diamond workshop on 47th Street, an area full of police. The Jew was gay, and the butterfly he lived with went around in a fright because who knows what the old man made him do. The victim approached Tuco: he closed the store at eight at night, turned out the lights, and then blew the fag. The deal was that the kid leaves the door open for us, we go in and seize the two with our guns concealed. And so it was. Eight at night in the summertime. Tuco carried my Falcon—which he'd fallen in love with—and I with his .38 revolver with a silencer. We went in. In order to leave the gay guy out of suspicion, Tuco pistol whipped him—he put a bloody gash on his head—and at the same time let the Jew knew that this was serious. But Jews being such thieves and so tight, the old man told us that he'd rather let us kill him than give us the gems. So I, who had to win Tuco's respect, grabbed the old man by the hair and threw him to the floor. I shot to kill, but, as I've always suffered from lousy aim, I didn't hit him. The shot kept right on going, went through the refrigerator door and broke a bottle of orange juice, which blew up with a really loud noise. The noise scared the Jew and he opened the strongbox for us: ninety thousand dollars in jewels. While Tuco was taking them out, I set about robbing rings and slipping them on every available finger. Tuco saw me and said, "Don't be a small-time thief, a punk from the streets; we got what we came for so put that trash down. We have to be decent, we have to work with style," while he dropped diamond after diamond into the small blue Chivas Regal bag he carried. For the big bag they gave us thirty thousand dollars, a third of what the diamonds were worth, but that's the international duty in Rio, Hong Kong, or London. Ten thousand for Tuco, ten thousand for me, and ten thousand for the gay guy who was a bloody mess.

We worked together for a while, because he had confidence in me, up until the day he told me he had a very risky job in San Francisco worth some ten million dollars. I told him that nothing fazed me. He replied, "Good, it's a question of an assault on a famous store that sells to all the big Hollywood artists." Tuco specialized in those. He called himself the tail of the comet because he lived just behind the stars. He laid out the operation for me. It seemed so easy that it made me suspicious. He saw it in my face and said that the only thing was a small problem of twenty flights, that there weren't elevators or escalators and we had to use suction cups like Batman. I got vertigo and had to sit down just so I could say no, not even for the devil himself; I would walk into a clean gunfight, but heights and I were longstanding enemies. No chance. We spoke frankly to each other. I am a man of the earth and water but not the air. To get on a plane I have to get drunk first and the whole trip I put my ear to the engine because I have the premonition that if it shuts off, down we go. ▓

I had been sending money to my wife and the kid I had with her to build up some savings. In six months I already had enough to retire on if I let myself go back to Colombia. I got to know the power of the dollar in the U.S., I learned English and developed a liking for maracachafa.[1] I dreamed about returning and, one day, without saying goodbye to anyone, I got on an Avianca flight headed to Miami, Barranquilla, and Bogotá. I flew directly to Leticia on a milk route that stopped in Villavicencio, Araracuara, Mitú, and La Pedrera. A voyage between two worlds.

I settled in rapidly in Amazonas.² I deposited my dollars in the Bradesco de Tabatinga Bank, bought a speedboat with a .220 motor, and went to live in El Cacao, an island outside Puerto Nariño, watching the river pass by and lighting my joints without the desire to do anything.

I stayed like that for awhile, letting my head wander wherever it liked. But solitude is a bad adviser and the desire for money doesn't leave you in peace. I put together a business called Silence Tours that I advertised in one of the best hotels in Leticia with a green and blue banner hanging on a table, manned by an Tucan Indian who I wouldn't let speak Spanish. The gringos arrived by the handful; we loaded them onto a canoe that the Indian sailed as far as the Yahuarcaca lakes, near Leticia, and then he turned off the motor and put out six oars for the tourists to take turns with while the Indian slept in a hammock slung in the stern. I paid the Tucan five dollars a day and charged each tourist twenty. A straightforward business.

On one of those trips I ran into an old friend from Australia whom I'd traveled with between La Havre and Sydney, passing through the Suez, when I was in the merchant marine. I got to know the sea when I was eighteen, when I entered the Naval Academy in Cartagena to become a noncommissioned officer. I stayed in military service for the obligatory period, and I hitched a ride on the first ship that set sail from Cartagena, for Rotterdam. Ships on the high seas are so boring that the best thing you can do is to work hard, sleep, and save up your energy so you can cut loose when you arrive in port. For that same reason there's a lot of gambling onboard, and it's serious stuff. Not always for money. One night I lost the advance that the purser had given me and I ended up owing the table 180 dollars. The winners met in private and told me that they would charge me the debt in services as a bodyguard through the red light district of Rotterdam. It seemed like a good deal to me, and when we disembarked we headed straight for the bars. While they danced and got drunk I kept an eye out for them without having the right to do cither of the two, but to the extent that they were drinking they were losing sight of me and I made my move on a chubby girl that everyone else ignored, even though she wasn't ugly. She ate me up with her eyes until I spoke to her, and when my patrons went out for their rounds, I proposed that we go for a room. She had big eyes, she was tiny, and she knew a few short words in Spanish. She let me know that she would go to bed with me, but in the dark; I accepted because you don't need light for that. We took off our clothes separately and I started to stroke her with the intensity you get after you've slept alone for two or three weeks out on the ocean. She liked it when I caressed the back of her neck and her thighs but she wouldn't let me touch her tits; definitely, the more we heated up, the more I forgot the rules and began to touch her all over, on all sides, passing from one tit to the other and from the other to the one and then the other and the other. One, another, and then one more. Three tits! Two the same size and a third hidden beneath the left tit. Three tits! I was afraid but having kissed them I became fond of all of them and said to myself, "Better a woman and a half than half a woman."[3] I liked her a lot. She didn't charge me because she said that normally when her clients discovered her extra tit they jumped up and tried to cheat her. She gave it to me as if it were nothing, she was that thankful. But what I saved in this encounter, the sailors, who were waiting for me in front of the room when I came out, charged me. The most expensive and most unusual sex I've ever had in my life: 180 dollars.

From Rotterdam to Le Havre and then to Sydney. My friend the Australian was a big guy: tall, around six feet, size twelve shoe, his hair in a ponytail in back, fifty years old.

Arthur. We became close friends because we shared the same bunk. He built sailboats and had sailed from Australia to Peru navigating by the stars. He went back to his house, assuring me that someday we would meet up again, because wanderers always travel the same roads. When I saw him in Leticia I couldn't believe the world had so few roads.

We drank several rounds of caipirinãs to celebrate meeting each other and then many, many bottles of Montilla rum, daydreaming first and later—with our heads in a mellow place—planning a trip between Leticia and Cairo. We formed a business, without worrying about who would do what, to build a sailboat and charter it. We would head out rowing in lashed-together canoes as far as Manaus, and there, using the best wood, we would build a sailboat to take us to Belém, through the mouth of the Amazon, cross the Atlantic, and drop anchor on the west coast of Africa. We would sell the boat so we could travel by land to Cairo and then head to Rome and Paris. Every day, from early until late, we talked and talked about the trip; I would supply the money, and he the experience, and along the way we would meet up with fellow travelers.

The first of September 1971, at five in the morning we shoved off from Amazonas with two Indians who helped us row and, most important of all, guided us. The river has many arms; if you choose the wrong one, you can lose one or two days and waste your energy. Our boat was made out of two canoes joined by a platform of wood where the stove was and where we hoisted the tent. All very simple, very primitive. When night fell we steered to the middle of the river and let ourselves be carried by the current where it wanted to take us. That's called sailing babaya. We woke up on a sand bank and went back to rowing all day. We arrived in Manaus with bloody hands and there, instead of building a sailboat, we bought one. Our desire to be on the open sea overpowered us, and in any case, Arthur couldn't find a hardwood that was light, strong, and resistant to water. It cost me sixteen thousand dollars, which I paid in cash. It was a hundred feet long, it cut the water like an arrow, and it seemed invisible. We baptized it the *Wind*.

Antonio—Brazilian, son of an Englishman and a Norwegian, born in Santa Helena, at the edge of the river, who had just arrived from a monastery in Nepal, where he'd spent five years—joined us. Further down, in Tepé, we met a gringo, a big racing car driver, who had driven in Indianapolis twice. He was enthusiastic about the trip, and, like a good gringo, he offered to buy the sailboat from us when we arrived in Africa, from where he would set out for Miami. In order to seal the deal he advanced me five thousand dollars. Arriving at Breve, another sailor asked to join up: Swiss, a champion sailor in the regattas on Lake Lemans. His name was Alain and he knew a lot about sailing.

Finally, in Portel a Spaniard from the Canary Islands slipped in with us. He was an expert about half the world without knowing how to do anything. He said people called him Vicente. Gathering up our adventurers we arrived at Belém do Pará twenty-eight days after setting sail from Manaus. There we stocked up on food and water for a crossing we figured could last between thirteen and fifteen days. We had agreed not to take women or alcohol, but we had a well-guarded container of herb.

When everything was ready we went to the harbormaster to get permission for the sail. They asked us for the sailboat's papers and those of the whole crew. The captain looked them over, examined them, compared them, and told us everything was fine but none of us had a sailor's license and therefore we couldn't set sail as we were. We talked among ourselves, analyzed the situation, and then decided to ask permission to try out the *Wind* while Arthur sent for his license in Australia. Nice guy, the harbormaster. We set out the twelfth of October to give the boat a spin as far as a nearby port named Vigía and, obviously, we never went back.

The first day was quiet. The second too. We were happy, nothing could stop us, we felt like we were dreaming. The night of the third day we started to hear something like a storm in the distance that didn't stop, a rustling coming out of a throat far away. It kept getting clearer and louder and by midnight, when it was pitch black, the noise was like thunder. We didn't understand that this was a fight between the Amazon and the Atlantic. The river opened up a passage of some three hundred miles of freshwater that pushed its way into the guts of the sea like a knife thrust. The ocean is, however, very observant; it doesn't take anything unusual into itself without its permission and throws everything back, be they trees, earth, ships, or shipwrecks. It hurls them back into the very same Amazon with such tenaciousness that before you arrive in the Atlantic you run into a countercurrent that pushes the river back with the might of the ocean. At exactly twelve midnight—because I looked at the clock—we heard an explosion, sharp and violent, that we knew without having to ask was dead serious. I thought that it was something to do with a piston on the motor—a motor so large that it had to be fired with a blowtorch before it started to run—but Arthur was able to tell us that we had rammed a tree below deck that hit us like a real torpedo, while Alain thought it was lightning because the impact produced a glow that lit up the river. The force of the wind in the unfurled sails, as strong as the power of the engine at full tilt, struck with the force of something thrown back by the sea.

We sank in twenty minutes; there wasn't a sound out of us; everyone knew it was the hour of death. I saw Arthur grabbing on to a mast, not knowing what the others did for themselves. I began to paddle like a dog, because all the ship's wood disappeared from my sight as if hell had swallowed it whole. I remembered that in the Naval Training Center at Barranquilla an instructor who was shipwrecked at Bocas de Ceniza told us that a man who is afraid of the water is the one who drowns. I tried to keep myself afloat without knowing which way was upstream and which way down; the night was so dark that it was all one whether my eyes were open or closed. In an instant everything had ended, as if I had died. Nothing happened: no thoughts, no feelings, no fear. Nothing. A hole in time, a part of life that passed without living it, a tunnel at the end of which was the end.

Dawn drew the traces of some sort of island that grew more solid as light filled the sky. I figured I needed to swim over a mile to get to it, despite the currents I was running into. I started to swim, trying to head toward the island that I supposed was—as it turned out to be—Marañón. But the brighter it got the more I gave up hope. Finally, when I let myself be carried where the river wanted, a tree trunk hit me on the head and I grabbed onto it with every bit of strength I had. I woke up on the beach. Like any castaway in any of the stories of any seas. It was soon dark again and I continued to sleep, or cry, until the following day, when I realized that hunger was becoming my enemy. I started walking, and by midday I saw some fishermen who greeted me as if I had fallen from the moon.

I told them what had happened to me and they didn't believe me, because smugglers use those channels all the time. I tried to make them understand my story but they were adamant I was a smuggler and for that reason, if they were going to take me to Belém, I had to pay them. I told them my story one more time and they almost laughed, until one of them said to me, "Look, we don't believe you but we can help you when we finish fishing, within five days."

I couldn't convince them. I had to endure the anguish of not knowing what happened to my companions until the fishermen brought me back to Belém, one step at a time, in their canoes. The anxiety was eating me alive. When we got to town I took off, without even saying goodbye, to file my report about the loss of the boat. But what could I report if everything I owned had sank, if I was nothing more than the cut-offs that an Indian had loaned me? Everything was at the bottom of the river: my money, my papers, my belongings. And so, without a single thing on me, I headed to the maritime police.

I was relating what had happened to me when, suddenly, I heard a familiar-sounding groan—it wasn't a voice. I looked to one side and then another and, in a cell on the other side of the room, I was able to make out Arthur's unruly head of hair, his big stonebreaker hands, his eyelashes flecked with dandruff over his always lively eyes: he was in jail for smuggling. The wretch didn't know how to speak anything but English and couldn't find a way to explain that we were going to cross the ocean. Her Majesty the Queen's consul was on vacation and that was why the authorities in Belém do Pará had the man in a cell. We saw each other, embraced, and broke down in tears. Then they believed us. They wished us well and called the newspaper *Folha do Norte* to have them take our photos and interview us. We were the only survivors. The others—Antonio, Vicente, Alain, Bob, the pilot, all of them—the river swallowed and never gave back.

I called my brother in Medellín. The dude had managed to slip several kilos into Miami and he was set. He told me, "Brother, I'll send you tickets, money, whatever you want right away." He wired me five hundred thousand pesos, which in those days was a lot of money. I wanted to blow all the bills in one shot, just like any successful and self-respecting outlaw. ▓

I went to stay with my sister, who was also living in Medellín. She was married to a much older engineer, with a big house in Robledo. I walked around by myself while I made plans to get an apartment for my wife. I hustled and made deals. A man over there has a car and a man here needs one? I put them together and took my commission. Someone had livestock and someone else had money? Don Someone meet Don So-and-So. And so it went. I liked this money game. I worked while I was sitting in the Café Ganadero, and there wasn't a day that something didn't happen.

During that time my sister invited me to a study group. I've always been lazy about books, but she said to me that it wasn't simply a question of books but of doing something for the country. "Or do you like the way we're headed?" she asked me. "Maybe you like it that the children are dying of hunger, that the people don't have work, that the campesinos are being thrown off their land?" "No," I told her, "I don't like that just like I don't like the sun going down, but it's none of my business."

The argument never ended. She insisted, "You who are so exceptional, with so much experience, so much intelligence to give to the fight, you don't believe that you can help the others?" She got to me by making me feel indispensable and then, well, you give in a little and end up reading *How the Steel Was Tempered,* a novel that tells the story of the struggle of a young communist during the First World War. In the study group we didn't discuss the books we were reading but somewhat more practical things. Fortunately. But in any case I found myself worn out reading Nikitin's *Political Economy,* Engles's *Principles of Communism,* Marx's *Manifesto,* Marta Harneker's *Principles of Historical Materialism,* and some article of Stalin's. It took me a lot of work to get through such a full cart, which had nothing to do with we were doing: painting slogans on the walls in the industrial areas, handing out propaganda, organizing demonstrations.

One day they invited me to write graffiti on some walls in Itagüí. It was the first time I went along and as always I threw a snub-nose .38 into the bag. A gun that my brother, the superbandit, had given me. We were painting the slogan "Fight on, Workers," when a security guard showed up. I took out the revolver, grabbed him by the neck, and threw him up against the wall. For me it was totally natural to neutralize a victim, but to those from the study group it was very cool and I started to get a reputation for being brave. I liked that. Little by little they didn't go anywhere without me, because I gave them security and to the extent that I won their confidence they let me know more closely what the group was up to. On the day that it was my turn to prepare an exposition on childhood prostitution, two things happened: my sister very mysteriously introduced me to a Spaniard who had just arrived from Cuba and a young woman named Vicky—or so they called her—joined the group. She looked at everything with an air of surprise; she had big dark eyes, long brown hair, and she always went around in a bathing suit with a beige trench coat. She didn't talk much, which I liked because that way I didn't have to invent an excuse every time I took her to my house. We walked around without saying a single word between us. We went out on the sly, giving little kicks to the stones, sometimes talking about the rain.

The Spaniard—he liked to be called Pablo—was another story. He liked talking about everything, the words didn't stay put in his mouth and he gave the impression of having very little time to say everything he wanted to say. He arrived with his page of life so crammed that it was hard work asking him anything. He was a tall man, white, with very powerful arms and eyes that were sharp and moved quickly. It was said of him without his saying it that he was the son of a Republican colonel exiled to France, an expert in gunpowder. Our hero had worked with the National Liberation Front of Algeria in Paris, where he became friends with Red Beard, the Cuban comandante in charge of organizing the people who arrived on the island for military training. In Cuba he was named to a high position in the Institute of Nutrition because, on top of everything he had said and done, he was a great chef. So good that he became Fidel's chef. Che gave him a Baretta with a marble grip and Ernest Mandel's *Treatise of Marxist Economy*, with a dedication that read, "May Cuba bring the defeat of the Invincible Armada." They let us know that he was an expert in plastic explosives and that he arrived in Colombia to organize the Armed Forces of Liberation, or AFL.

I started to like the study circle when these two came in. Pablo was a master from whom one could learn a great deal and Vicky a mysterious child with whom I liked to walk around. Both of them were trying to get me on their side because they couldn't stand each other. He invited me to his hideaway to tell me histories that blew my mind: the organization of the International Brigades during the Spanish Civil War; the Algerian attacks on the French; the daily life of Fidel and Che. He had a catalog of modern weapons of war that detailed the make, model, and caliber, range, shots per second, different types, the way to take them apart, and the names of the parts. He gave us an introductory course on weapons and then another more thorough one on plastic explosives. He kept a notebook written by hand in blue and red ink that became our bible, even though he only gave it to us in his presence. The illustrations were very elaborate and they looked to me to be very clear and scientific. From the pleasure I was getting learning from him I became his secretary, or class monitor; and while he explained the mechanisms of, for example, the Colt .45 pistol I held it up, unloading and loading it with only one hand in less than a minute. While all this was happening, Vicky went about her things. Since she didn't talk much, I was satisfied seeing her just on the afternoons or weekends. Pablo, his weapons and his convictions, took up the rest of my time.

One day, within the confines of the explosives course, he called on a few of us and, without much introduction but very solemnly, told us that in order to graduate as authentic revolutionaries we had to move from theory to practice, showing us the necessity of escaping from the vicious circle we were trapped in: "We don't have guns because we don't have money and we don't have money because we don't have guns." He proposed that we take firearms from those who had them: the cops.

We carried out our first attack, which we called Violeta. It was a question of making a direct assault on the first police officer we met and taking his revolver and uniform. He taught us to make "rolls" with zinc tubes covered with rubber sleeves. Four of us went out one night with Pablo. I was used to using real guns so the whole thing struck me as between ridiculous and foolish but, in any case, the chance to do something more useful than reading books attracted me. So we went out on the hunt and in a little while we came across a big fat cop who was getting off a bus. We followed him. Pablo and I were the ones with the job of surprising him but at the decisive moment my companion separated from the group and I was on my own. It fell to me to give the poor policeman a handful of tubing that we hadn't planned. I had to be sure about it. The others helped me. We disarmed him and stripped him. Pablo told us later what we had done, or actually what we hadn't done, went toward part of the course that measured our capacity for improvisation. But I was still doubtful and he began to feel it when we decided to organize the operations on our own. We became the terror of Medellín's police; in six months we got our hands on 113 small arms. We were so hard on them that we even started to like them. We handed the pistols over to Pablo and he sent them to a group that was organizing in the Perijá range.

I no longer believed anything he said. Neither what he had done nor what he could do, and little by little we lost the confidence that we had in him. Until one day he disappeared. Six months later they tore him up with a machine gun in an encounter with the army. The press wrote that that they had to cut off his hands in order to make him submit to finger printing at the Popayán Battalion. I felt guilty for having distrusted his involvement and I cried for many days.

The group was gaining confidence in its military operations and, at the same time, we were abandoning our studies. Without letting go of thinking about her, I didn't go back to seeing Vicky. From the cops we moved on to the banks, and at the end of an action against the Commerce Bank on 70th they surrounded us and we had to get away by means of some clean shots.

It turns out that I had a '53 Willys nicknamed Sebastian that started only when it wanted. That time, like always, I had parked it nearby, on a small hill, in order to roll it down if it didn't want to start. When the gun battle broke out we ran to get Sebastian and, of course, the engine didn't turn over. We hunched down to push it in the middle of the gunfire and right away I felt a hot current in my chest. I shouted, "They've hit me!" but since I kept on pushing, everyone thought I was just talking shit. Finally Sebastian cooperated and we jumped in without letting up on the shots. As we got away a round of fire reached us and a tire blew out: we were moving on three wheels, throwing off sparks at one hundred miles per hour because the tire had come off the rim; I drove with just one hand since I had to cover the hole that the shot had opened with my other hand, while a red tube hung out of my stomach, making bubbles every time I breathed. No one took any notice of my wound while we were moving and absorbed in the gunfight. We were still driving like mad when news of the assault and the dead guy came over the radio. That was me. From that day on they called me "Dead Man" and, for a nickname, "Puppet."

When we arrived at the hideout they dressed my wound. The shot had entered on the side and had gone out by the nipple. Luckily, it only grazed the heart but it took a piece of the lung with it. The bullet managed to take a little bit along to the other side of the skin. Remembering a film called *Butch Cassidy*, I asked for hot water and a sheet, pushed the intestine back in with my finger, cleaned myself and tied myself up tight. I called my sister and told her what happened without giving details. When she arrived I was just about dead; I couldn't see colors and I almost wasn't breathing. She took me to a clinic, telling them that a stray bullet wounded me. The doctor called F-2,[4] and, at the exit to the operating room where they sewed me up, a captain was waiting for me.

"You bastard. What were you mixed up in?"

"Nothing, captain. A stray shot."

"A stray shot? Just like the one they fired at the cop left for dead on 70th street? Don't insult me!"

My sister handed me over to the captain and the judge had orders to move me from the clinic to the jail after three days. On the second day Pedrito, a faithful and lively friend, showed up with a gun and said, "Let's go, brother," and he made his way out with nobody's permission, in spite of the cops who were guarding me. Pedrito was the bravest and boldest of us all; he was an excellent marksman and he didn't talk shit or boast. A few days later another companion killed him. I was cleaning my wound in the bathroom when I heard a single, clean shot. Strange. I went out and arrived in time to see Pedrito falling over. Pablo had taught us to use the revolver just above the waist and we played Fastest Draw to find out who drew his gun and fired the fastest. Pedro was always the winner and for that reason everybody wanted to measure themselves against him, until the devil grabbed the gun from Dionisio and killed Pedrito. It was awful to see him dead and sad to have to wrap him up in a rug and throw him into the Medellín River, without burying him and without paying respects. What a shame, Pedrito. You were so beautiful, always ready for anything.

The deaths of Pablo and Pedrito demoralized me. I couldn't lift my head. I couldn't stop thinking about Pablo's hands and the look of surprise on Pedro's face when he realized that the game was serious and that his friend, Dionisio, had killed him. I thought that we were going about doing something evil and wrong because so much error couldn't happen by chance. When death is hanging over you, you have to stop and take a good look at what is happening and where things are going. Death has its way of making itself known, but sometimes you cover your eyes and ears so that she does what she wants with you. I started looking for Vicky again; her silence gave me security and studying with her helped me overcome my fear. We read all the time. She taught me to enjoy Neruda, Benedetti, Hernández, Vallejo, Alberti. Now we knew that the manuals smacked of shit.

I didn't go back to spending time with my companions and, even though I was hanging out with Vicky, I went back to live with my wife and my son Danilo, who was now three years old. She was pregnant again and gave birth to a daughter we baptized Esperanza. Every afternoon I would meet Vicky in Versalles, we drank juice made from mandarin oranges and walked through Junín as far as La Playa. Later we climbed up to the Pablo Tobón Theater, always talking about the day when all the ceiba trees would be gone and only the busts of Antioquia's greatest sons would remain. I went with her on her errands too, about which I never dared to ask her anything. I went back to the Café Ganadero, to keep my antenna up for any deals. I was living the quiet life, everything seemed to have settled down and I could almost accept growing old as I closed in on my thirtieth birthday.

Sebastian had been lost the day of the big shootout but nobody paid any attention to him and I was able to get him back. I sold him and bought a '52 Ford van with a large storage area; I souped it up to the max, installed a double carburetor and the best sound system outside of a listening booth. On the afternoon of June 16, 1973, Vicky asked me if I could go with her as far as Puerto Valdivia to deliver a supply of screws to the Purveyor Hardware Store, and, since she was also making deals, it seemed a very natural thing to me. We went.

We were talking about the earth overheating when she said to me, "I know you're a tough type and that's why I want to tell you that what we're carrying in the storage in back isn't screws but guns." "Guns?" I asked her. "Bang-bang guns?" And she answered, with a big smile on her face, "Absolutely, bang-bang guns." The truth was, it didn't matter to me; I'd seen more dangerous things on other occasions. So, plucking up my courage and living up to my fame, I kept driving as if nothing had happened. To reassure myself, I took out my .38 with its new barrel and laid it next to me. Driving past Puerto Valdivia, before the crossing at Tarazá, she told me to make a right turn. We were going along a narrow road when suddenly I see the military reserve in the middle of the road. I told her, "Vicky, get yourself together because I'm going to stop. Have the gun ready." I slowed the car down as if obeying the army checkpoint and when the soldier came close I put the car in gear and floored it: we went over the hill in the middle of the bullet fire we'd brought on. I crouched down while Vicky fired and we kept going without knowing how. I know that I didn't kill any soldiers but I also know that at least two have to get around in wheelchairs.

They started coming after us right away. I revved up the engine at the top of the hill to make it sound like we were taking off. I said to Vicky: "We can't give these weapons to the army so let's throw them into the Cauca." Which we did. I hurried to clean the finger prints off the steering wheel with a rag without remembering that the owner's papers were in my name. I laughed inside because on the outside I was, de facto, joining the guerrillas. We abandoned the car and set out to cover the hill on foot. We walked the whole night almost without speaking. I didn't reproach her at all; actually I was overwhelmed by the games destiny plays with you. But it is what it is and there's nothing you can do about it. So, on to the mountain, Puppet! ▓

To go into the mountains and make contact with the guerrillas wasn't easy. The army had mounted a concentric circle with various rings, and we were outside trying to break in to meet up with the people and then later break through with them to get out. There was no other way. We were moving inside the circle; the very presence of the army told us where the guerrillas were travelling and where we shouldn't go. Finally, after almost two days of dodging the enemy, we managed to squeeze through. A comrade in arms recognized Vicky and showed us the positions. I embraced everything we encountered because, really, the meeting is very emotional. The war makes everything more vivid, the heart beats faster and each minute is longer. A patrol took us to the lookout, one Hector, who treated me like an old friend; he spoke privately with Vicky and sent us to headquarters. The man in charge was named Helio, a skinny dude who also greeted me in a very strange way, which I couldn't make up my mind was a welcome or a congratulation. Every single thing behind the lines has something to say and you become very agile at understanding what lies behind each word. Helio sent us to the mess hall, because he could see that we were extremely hungry and there they gave us, without more ado, guns. They knew who I was because Vicky had told them everything; I on the other hand didn't know what she was involved in. But to make the best out of a bad situation, without reproaches or explications, I accepted what befell me.

The first thing, clearly, was to get out of the circle. Helio separated us; he sent Vicky—who in the woods was known as Patricia—to join a team of doctors and me to his second in command, Comandante

Tarquino. From the first he seemed to me a arrogant person. A cold bastard. He gave orders in such a way that everything showed off his superiority.

Being separated from Vicky hit me hard. I felt like they had torn off my arm, my leg, and then to top it off my mother had abandoned me in the hospital. I shared the guerrilla's ideals. I had pledged my life for those ideas in the city and if I had left them behind it was my own choice. But now I felt obligated to fight, and things lose passion that way. That's why right from the start I told Tarquino that I had come there by accident; that they could be sure of my honesty and commitment but I hadn't agreed to stay there and I wanted to leave when it was considered convenient.

A few days after having broken through the rings Helio called on me. He turned out to be an understanding guy. He told me that he had heard a lot about me and that he trusted me but if I didn't want to stay in the woods I could easily leave when we got close to the Magdalena River. So it was. Fifteen days later, in a Johnson, they took me to Magangué. I never saw Vicky again.

From Magangué I left for Barranquilla. I didn't have any money and didn't want to arrive at the house broke after having been gone without even saying good-bye. I remembered a friend known as Mi Gente who owed me a favor. I went looking for him. He was wealthy, retired. He welcomed me to his house, gave me the keys to his BMW to use as I wanted, and introduced me to a German, a Nazi official from the Second World War who lived in semiseclusion in Calamar. A sharp man. Informed about everything, from repairing the engine of a plane to playing one of Beethoven's sonatas, but he hadn't been able to learn Spanish. It was very difficult to understand what he said. When I met him he was making sauerkraut with cabbage that he'd grown himself. I started to beat around the bush because it pained me to propose something to such a respectable person but Don Berth, as he was called, gave me a look with his eyes that cut the discussion short. He said, "Mi Gente doesn't send me anything but rogues. You are here for a pound of salt, so tell me where it is, when, and how we are going to distribute the spoils. Let's call things by their name." He said it to me in German, and he later translated it for me to something like the same language.

"Pound of salt?" I kept asking myself. "What's he talking about?"

I thought it must be code. Mi Gente had told me, "Don't listen to him, he's a strange man; better you pay attention to the following business. We're each getting a third: one part for me for making the connection; one part for him for his work, and the other part for you for distracting the night watchman in a store on 33d Street. The German doesn't like scandal, blood, or violence; those are his conditions; and then, afterward, my good friend, you have to work with silk gloves so you get the watchman out of the way as smoothly as possible. One more thing: the old man took a bayonet to one eye and he can't see anything through his glass eye, which nobody notices because it looks almost real. So don't stand on his right side but to his left, so he doesn't get pissed off."

But no matter how much I went over and over my conversation with Mi Gente carefully, I couldn't figure out the code for a pound of salt. I had to call him on the phone and ask him what this little game was about. Mi Gente said, "Don't bother yourself with superficial shit and trust the man." ▓

On the day of the job we met at the restaurant in the Hotel Prado, all of us elegantly dressed, as he had demanded. Don Berth ordered sweet and sour pork chops with two beers and corn bread. He told me to ask for the same. We left around ten at night. We got out of the BMW near the store, which was located on the second floor; he asked me to please go in first, get the watchman out of the way, and, when everything was ready and quiet, turn the light on and off twice to signal them. I did everything to the letter. The watchman didn't even let out a grunt. He realized what was happening when he was already bound and gagged in the bathroom, with his head in the basin and his hands tied behind the toilet. I told him not to make any noise and called to my German, who arrived like a doctor when he's going to operate: steady and silent. From his leather briefcase, which he must have had with him throughout the war, he took out a black cloth, the famous pound of salt, and a glass container. He asked me for water, filled the bottle, spread out the pound of salt, submerged two electric cables, made dough with one and with the other lit a small acetylene torch which he held over the combination lock on the strong box, covering the sparks and the light with the black cloth. The lock started to melt tear by tear, while he talked to me about the Valkyries. An hour holding forth; an hour of clean work. They killed him later in Medellín, in one of those slaughters the police know how to pull off.

We didn't get much money, but it was more than enough to stir me up and go back to working on my own. Mi Gente gave me the address of a pawnshop in Barranquilla, owned by a Turk famous for being a miser. The man went back to his house early and left a poor dude locked inside with a thermos of red wine filled to the brim. The first thing I had to do was go for the Turk in his house. I grabbed him by the neck and obliged him to open the store. I let the employee know that, if he moved, I would kill him. I didn't need to say it to the Turk because he knew. In the middle of the man's wailing I started to throw watches and jewelry into a bag. One score after another, and when I was ready to take off the Turk grabbed hold of the sack weeping, begging me to kill him, kill him, but don't take the stuff. I kicked him and told him to wise up until I got disgusted seeing him stoop so low, debasing himself and more than anything else weighing so much, because added to the watches it was an impossible load with the man pulling in the other direction. I lost control of myself and I shot him three times, until he let go. I don't know if I killed him, but I know I wanted to.

I went back to Medellín to live with my wife and my children. My intention to make amends was sincere and I wanted to make a break from the life I was leading. Living vicariously wears you out because, after a while, what in the beginning is new gets old, familiar, the same. I needed to take shelter under a wing, like a little chicken; I wanted them to accept and forgive me. There are moments when you need to be pardoned, even if you haven't done anything bad; at times you feel the weight of solitude that you are carrying around hidden like freedom. I went to live with the whole family in a hotel because I couldn't bear my wife's parents; they charged too high a price in *Please, may I's* to live with them.

I went out at eight in the morning to work; I mean, to look for what I could scrounge up, like a street punk, an outlaw, or a *gentleman*. In the street, face to face with hunger, all those names mean nothing more than ways to live, to get over on the other person. Very conveniently, I accommodated myself to the convenience of having the revolver resting against my belly, there where you can feel its weight, and I went out to look the day straight in the eyes. Every person is an opportunity; you have to study every one of them, and when you run into one you have to get the better of them just like that. Without disgust and without heart. I went back to working the "Don't say a word," above all in stores and the apartment buildings of the wealthy and the tourists. But the payoff was small and the risk great. To keep working as a bandit I had to put together my own gang and that in the long run is the same place that fosters informants. You have to wake up every day thinking where will I be seized today, who do I have to jump over, and at bottom this fear of not returning at night, this fear that the eyes of your children you said good-bye to while they slept in the morning will wake up crying over you on the way to the morgue—that made me feel like shit. Better that they kill you over there in the corner, where no one can see it, and let your children cry for you when you're already in the ground.

That's why I thought about finding the one thing all of us were looking for. I had made a connection and, following up on it, I arrived in southern Cauca to buy basuco.[5] I knew that in Cartagena, where the good people go to do things that aren't so good, there's a big market for basuco. It cost me some effort to find a decent person who knew how to get his hands on it; no one knew, no one had heard anyone talk about it, no one paid attention even to listen to offers. But finally the monkey came out to dance when he heard the coins and I ran straight into the knife. One Melquisadec, a campesino, invited me out to his spread and there, with much hocus pocus, poured a dark beige powder from out of a box that he kept hidden inside his bedclothes. He let me try some and I, the ingenious one, the hard type, he who knew everything, took a spoonful, a candle, and put on a show of the test: melting the basuco, separating out the oil, then smelling it to ascertain its purity, its strength, its taste. A true professional.

"Very good, yes, it's fine. How much do you have?"

"Just a little here, but I can get up to one hundred kilos for you."

"OK," I answered, just like I was an old donkey.

A little later I was traveling in a Rapid Guachicono bus with my duffel bag of basuco. I arrived in Cali and took a plane to Cartagena. Everything was fine. I went into the hotel, called Mi Gente, told him I had high-quality merchandise and needed to connect with his network of dealers. We made arrangements, and a little later a big black guy with an ugly face arrived with an American girl. She had light brown hair, and was supersexy and supercool. I gave them some to try while they asked me about the price per kilo and examined the quality. Once they'd seen it, they made a face that said no. But they looked it over thoroughly, melting it with the heat of their fingers and smelling it, and then with an infallible authority they told me, "It doesn't pass the test. We're sorry but they tricked you; it's dried banana, ground up with a little acid sprinkled on top so it smells."

Melquisedec had got the better of me. The anger I felt wasn't so much for the swindle as for my presumption of being an expert judge. I felt like a fool. Like a total fool, tricked by a campesino from Bolivar, Cauca, a village that nobody knows if it exists or not and it doesn't matter to anyone either way.

I made a return call on the piggy bank of problem solvers, Mi Gente.

"Man, Puppet," he told me, "You'll always be the same. The guerrillas softened up your brains. Who told you to trust a campesino? But all right then, get yourself to Buenaventura, look for So-and-So, and buy high quality 'French cut' that will do to mix the coca and add to its weight. This time, I'm selling you the flour to see if you get out of being poor. And an idiot."

Said and done. In Buenaventura I bought a powder that the seller didn't know exactly what it was and he called simply "French cut." He sold it to me for very little and that gave me the feeling that it wasn't "cut." My suspicions turned into fear as I thought about the face of

Mi Gente calling me an idiot one more time. I was losing my standing with the man and that's a very serious thing, because without one's reputation the possibilities for doing real business go way down. I separated out a bit and sent it to the people at Bolivar University to study. I had a friend there who turned green when the laboratory tests concluded it was heroin. No more nor less. I made a nice pile with her because, as the saying goes, I spent ten and earned ten thousand.

I gave in to the impulse to do what I always do when I score: I went to Amazonas. Leticia was different now. It had a lot of energy, deals, speed. The people went from here to there, busy; the friends who were starting out when I had left were now all rich, extremely rich. The authorities very cunningly let them work, and when the merchandise arrived they made several agreed upon seizures and the cocaine went right back up. It worked for everybody. I thought about doing business, but at the hour of truth I discovered that the best business was in being a "little hump" and living off commissions. Hard work. Dangerous. But very well paid. I hired a few brave gunmen and set them to enforcing the agreements, fulfilling the laws that the bandits have in order to be able to do business: pay on time, respect one's word, don't fulfill the law halfway, be willing to take the consequences.

My work was much appreciated and I decided that they would pay me in merchandise, because I had been stung by the vice of smuggling. I wanted to make my own shipments so I wasn't working for the big shots for free. I thought about it, looking at it from one angle and then another because it was a very treacherous move in a world I didn't know well. But the worm gets inside you and settles down in its own command post. And just like that, little by little, I scored.

In New York I had met a gringo pilot who had worked with the CIA and participated in the invasion of the Bay of Pigs. He knew the Caribbean like his own hands, didn't take life seriously, chewed gum, and whatever he ate he always had ketchup on his hand. I called him from Leticia and we made a date in Miami, where he lived with two women for whom, beside a swimming pool, he had built identical houses and was building a third for himself, because he said that he was growing old. Ricky had been a boxer and it was obvious that he could kill a bull with one blow. I didn't have to insist: two daiquiris and his leather cap started to get sweaty. We made a deal: two parts for him and three for me, always and whenever I came with the shipment. We failed to set up a connection in the U.S. but, as always, for that there was Mi Gente.

We met up in different public places. In New Orleans we drank for two days because carnival was in progress, a celebration for black people that, like all their celebrations, consists in getting up in white or black costumes and then heading down to the street. Jazz was in the air day and night; there were bands that simply didn't stop, they lived playing music nonstop: they ate, slept, and made love in close quarters with their sad, contagious, and mischievous music; a music that gambles with freedom and fear. The living statues really impressed me: a being—neither man nor woman—who didn't bat an eyelash, didn't inflate their chest to breathe, and on whom you couldn't even detect a pulse. Perfectly still, but then, suddenly, when you are looking at them wide-eyed, they blink their eye, only to go on staring at nothing afterward.

In one of those narrow, capricious streets I fell in love with a Colombian from Armenia. A quiet girl, she had deep, flashing eyes and dark chestnut hair that she let hang loose. I learned later she was a poet. She said everything with her breath and the sweat of her hands. Her gaze looked inward, at times with teary eyes. I loved her very much and gave her a pearl necklace I had stolen. In between her two tennis shoes, which were old and falling apart, she left me a poem that has traveled with me ever since:

After so many attempts at loving each other
slowly,
awakening ourselves while shunning the prince and princess
slipping away from the mirrors, the braids
and the threads,
at washing our hands of children
gambling against the womb

and conjuring against fear, silence, and desire
you come to break the spell
with paradise on your back
and the fires of hell between your legs.

We flew to Kingston so we could get through the carnival hangover and wouldn't have to go to work right away. Two days on the beach to put distance between us and New Orleans and then indeed, right away, to Leticia by way of La Guajira and Vichada. We landed without trouble at the Vásquez Cobo Airport. While the plane, a two-engine Navajo of I don't know how many horsepower that could fly between Riohacha and Miami without refueling, was getting maintenance, I squared up with the authorities with a bit of small change and on Monday the twenty-first of June at seven in the morning we set off straight for Puerto Estrella in Guajira, to refuel there and, flying over Cuba, to land in an orange grove owned by a Colombian near Fort Noy.

Until Puerto Estrella the flight was monotonous. We were reserving our energy for the step over the Caribbean. Ricky brought along a pound of gum, and I a book of crossword puzzles, to entertain ourselves and keep ourselves from thinking what we were doing or what could happen to us. We were carrying nearly sixty kilos of the prettiest crystal I've ever seen. We flew three times around the salt markings that serve as an airport in Puerto Estrella, so that the police would recognize us, and then we dropped down for gas. We went back into the air with a confidence that gave me a bad back. You have to consider what could go wrong for things to turn out right.

The day was clear, the motors hummed along, we followed the flight plan to a T. Intermittent cumulous clouds forced us to change our course a few kilometers, but in general we flew in a straight line. We asked permission to fly over the extreme eastern end of the island of Cuba but the Communists refused permission categorically and we had to fly over Haiti. We had just lost it from view when I heard the engine cough. I was frozen with fear. I looked at Ricky, who opened his window and spit out the gum. The motor went back to coughing.

Ricky pushed the visor of his leather cap up with his index finger, sat back down in his seat and we started to climb straight up, as if we were going to meet God himself. The plan climbed and climbed and that son of a bitch of a motor coughed and coughed until it shut down. I looked at the motionless propeller. "At last we're up there," Ricky said and he pointed to the altimeter: two thousand feet. It was cold. "Hold on," he added, and we let ourselves go to the sky below with our heads pointing straight at the ocean.

The idea, as the man explained it to me in the middle of our terror, was to get the water that had leaked into the carburetor out, "using the Law of Gravity." I didn't understand, that much was clear, but at least I realized that I was wrong in thinking that the plan was to go very high up so we could angle ourselves from there, sloping downward until we arrived in Florida.

In any case, we didn't have much room for idle talk at that moment. We went down further and further without the motor starting up again. The ocean was visible below us, closer and closer every second. I touched the Lugar that, luckily, I had strapped on—against Ricky's orders—and said to myself, "I'll die before the big splash." But so what, you can't bring yourself to do it. The propeller on the coughing engine was still paralyzed and Ricky started to sweat. The waves of the sea and their white crests were already visible when ta-ta-ta-ta-ta-ta-ta . . . the small engine had dislodged the water and kicked into action. We returned to our horizontal position and Ricky threw three sticks of gum into his mouth without tearing off the papers. I, for my part, threw the Lugar out the little side window as a sign of thanks.

Quiet came back to break up the game. The noise of the engine lulled us—and then knocked us out—in one of those two P.M. molasses-heavy states of drowsiness. I was still asleep when Ricky gave me a hard slap on the thigh. Half peeling my eyes, I struggled to see Florida far off in the distance. I slapped Ricky on the shoulder and said, "Welcome home." Then he hit me a second time and pointed with his index finger to a sight just outside the window: a Phantom plane from the gringo air force. A black plane, almost soundless, manned by a pilot in goggles and headset who looked like a giant fly.

He was authoritatively sending signals that were incomprehensible for me but not for Ricky, who was receiving other orders over the radio to give his identification, route, and more data I didn't understand, and then afterward to land at the Miami airport. The Phantom moved up and away and a second later it was on our left side; then it flew up again and went ahead of us, flying in patterns, until Miami came into view and in the middle of the city, sitting there like an open mouth that was going to eat us, the airport. We got closer bit by bit and lost altitude while the Phantom hovered in order to keep an eye on us. Ricky made contact with the control tower and gave them the information they needed for landing.

The runways were visible below and the Phantom above. The highways on the boundaries of the airport were full of cars. We circled the airport while they gave the permission to land, which I took advantage of to tell my friend, "Be calm, brother, you don't know anything. I hired you for ten thousand dollars. Don't budge from that. I will pay whatever is required." But he was thinking about something else: he aligned himself with the runway and was headed toward it, but suddenly, in one quick movement, he put the plane over the highway—I believe he lost his mind—and then lower, lower, he found an open lane and boom! that's where he landed. The cars pitched themselves to either side, crashing into each other; at the end we hit the pavement and bounced up and down until the small plane came to a stop. We jumped out and took off running, each of us on our side, but there wasn't anywhere to go because the highway was enclosed by two fences: one that separated it from the airport and the other from a sewer. To put it simply, trapped like two mosquitoes in a spider's web. We spent three, four, or five minutes listening to police sirens and many more listening to "Get down on the ground!"

And to the ground we went. A huge policeman with bulging muscles put his boot on my neck and, being a real prick, left it there. A very pretty cop, tiny with dark hair, told him quietly that I was going to suffocate, but the man didn't move at all. It was the first engagement for a new force, made up of police, the army, and the navy, which Vice President Bush himself had baptized Stars and Bars, which is like calling a battalion of Colombian cops "O Unfading Glory." When one of those monsters—whom it's not worth calling a son of a bitch or anything else—was putting the handcuffs on me, he did it so roughly I screamed in pain. They lined us up against the flanges of our little plane, put the chains on us with the cocaine at our feet, and let the newspapers at us. Lights, cameras, questions, *show*. I said to myself, "Puppet, you've crashed into twenty years at least; you're thirty-two, plus twenty equals fifty-two; you'll get out of this part of the trip while you're still alive. You're not going to lower your head in front of these monkeys, neither are you going to crash, because you went to a really tough school; your dead friends and your people have gone on ahead. If you talk the devil will take you, because not even the enemy respects an informer. Keep yourself locked tight and bear up under what's coming to you." Yes, sir, and from there on I didn't shrink from their gaze or talk to them. The photographs were published in the *Miami Herald* and *El Colombiano*.

They transported us to Hunter Air Base, where a good number of colonels and generals came to look us over, like we were strange animals. We were two crazy people on display: they didn't interrogate us but instead analyzed us. After a little while I repeated to Ricky what I'd said before. "Be calm, friend, I'll take the fall. You don't know anything. Just tell them that we loaded up in Leticia, flew to Guajira, and then to Miami. Keep your mouth good and closed and I'll carry the weight."

From the air base they took us to the house jail, an inspector's office where the specialists who soften people up do their interrogations. First a crushing cell, two by two, isolated, without light, only a metal cot and a basin. They opened it, I walked in, and they shut it. The harsh sound of doors closing and the guards' indifference—they didn't even look at me—made me feel like the most abandoned person in the world. The cell didn't have a single trace of humanity, not even a mark on the wall, a sign, or smoke from a candle. Nothing. Just straight lines. Only a cockroach, an enormous cockroach that fed on the same things that make the gringos grow, stood motionless staring at me, vibrating its antennae; then it ran on its little racetrack and went back to standing quietly in place. I was staring at it when the federal cops arrived. They took me to a room where there was a lightbulb and a chair—like in the movies—sat me down, and started the inquisition. I was wearing some fancy shoes I had bought on my first trip, boots worth the foolish little sum of 680 dollars, and they started from there: why did I have boots like that; had I already been in Miami, when, where, and why, what had I been doing, what about this, what about that. Very little about coke. Two hours, three hours, four hours, until they started to catch up in the direction of the shipment: where did they leave from, where did they get the coke, who came up with the money, where were they taking it, who was going to sell it. Another four hours.

The following day I was taken to the Metropolitan Correctional Center. Another cell like the one before, rectangular and white but without the cockroach. Then to court. The judge with his cap and robes, the witness stand, and cross-examination. Every question that the man asked me I took as an opportunity to tell my story from when I was a child, the conditions under which I was raised, the life of my country, the violence and poverty. I was painting a canvas much larger than that of the crime I had committed. I spoke in my English, exaggerating my *misteics* along the way. The judge corrected me, I thanked him, and just so we were becoming like teacher and student. Little by little I was getting the upper hand. There was also a secretary who transcribed everything I said on a small, odd-looking typewriter. She was a mature woman, but still pretty. Her eyes had an anguished look, as if they had seen too much. When I exited the court room, someone called out to her and I grasped that it was to tell her about the birth of her first grandchild. All right, I said, the worm gets another morsel thrown its way.

The next day, the first thing I did was to ask about her grandchild. She looked astonished and told me that it was a boy, he was beautiful, and they had named him Lynn. "Beautyfull," I told her, and she sat there looking at me with so much thankfulness that it made even me feel good. The judge decided, in his wisdom and thanks to my statements, to set Ricky free on two thousand dollars bail. Me they remanded to trial. I went back to my cell and to the witness stand. Mi Gente had hired a superlawyer for me, Clark McCollin, the same lawyer who later worked for Noriega. At that time the gringos didn't have practice with us Colombians. They passed on my history to the judge and my questions about her grandson to the secretary. I successfully convinced the first that for a Colombian like myself, accustomed to misery and violence, a prison in the United States was paradise and that the sentence was a greater punishment for my wife and children. The secretary did her part and helped me a lot. In short, the judge delivered the sentence: for conspiracy four and a half years, for the importation of cocaine another four and a half years, and for landing on the highway the same. I was counting: four and half, nine, thirteen and a half, when suddenly there was a pause, he looked at me and said, "Concurrently," that is to say, with one of the four and a half years I would simultaneously be serving the other four and a half and the other four and a half. In other words, only four and a half years! I, who thought I was going to serve fifteen years for each crime. I exited in handcuffs but happy. The judge made a public statement that he was sorry to have to "condemn a victim of a despotic and corrupt system such as exists in Colombia." I completely agreed. The lawyer congratulated me and told me that in reality I had left him without a job.

But not completely. They condemned me to serve my sentence in the Memphis, Tennessee jail, a high-security prison, or, to put it another way, a cage for the worst, the most dangerous and most murderous, after I had spent eight months in the Correctional Center, which was a club. The day that I was shipping out to Memphis, I saw my pilot Ricky coming in: they had caught him with a shipment of eight tons of marijuana.

They handcuffed me to another gringo, a redheaded monkey who didn't say a word the entire trip and who didn't move once. They threw us in with all the others who were going to Tennessee in a windowless van, chained hand and foot. If I wanted to take a piss I had to take the monkey with me and I went with him when he wanted to shit. To eat we had to squat down. That's how they go about alienating you. The guards kept us from looking each other in the eye and from speaking among ourselves. They limited themselves to giving harsh orders in a few words, which felt like a hammer hitting your bones. But, in spite of everything, I kept thinking that I could do the four and a half years while dancing. If twenty years is nothing, like the tango says—and the tango comes from Antioquia—how are four years going to screw me over? We stopped in Tallahassee, a third-level prison, and going in I saw two prisoners being set free.

Then Memphis. At the entrance they read us the regulations for the cells in the High Security prison where we were going: sun every eight days, for two hours in the courtyard; a shower every forty-eight hours, for five minutes; the same food every day; a clean cell, inspection every twelve hours; punishment cell—the Dog House—to pay for any infraction. "It is absolutely prohibited to talk with the other prisoners," the director warned us. "And now, you start to make amends for the damage you have done to society, to the United States, and its government."

The cells were completely isolated. Walls, roof, and floor made out of metal; no communication possible with the cell next door; a bed, a toilet, a metal desk bolted to the wall, with two sheets of paper and a tiny lead pencil, as big as the small joint on your pinky. I knew that large pencils were used as weapons and they had been completely banned because a prisoner had snuck up on another inmate who was asleep, put the pencil inside his ear, and then given him a blow with his shoe that destroyed his brain.

I took care of my pencil and paper, writing letters to my children with very short sentences, telling them about the beautiful things in the United States and how happy I was working for them in a factory. From Colombia came letters written down by their mother. But not a word from her. She didn't have to do it for me.

One Saturday I went out for my sun break. I was leaning up against the wall when two huge guys stepped right in front of me. One told the other that he was going to kill him. I stopped breathing and didn't move. The other replied no, please don't do it, but the first had no compassion: he stabbed him without looking at me. The dying man was falling down, as he went on talking to himself, doubling over until he landed at my feet. Right away the guards appeared and without a word carried me off to the Dog Jail: a jail inside the other jail, where they put the extremely deranged, the sexual predators, and the Mariel Cubans.[6] Stripped naked, they stuffed me into a straitjacket tied around the waist. All I could hear was the cries of the poor madmen locked up there like dogs, under artificial light night and day. It's said that once upon a time a commission from the bureau of prisons made an inspection and a Cuban exile bit off his testicles and hurled them at the commissioners so they could get an idea of the conditions they were being held in.

Another Cuban told me he wasn't a worm,[7] a defector, that he had been born a socialist and he was a socialist, but that with the itch for adventure he'd thrown his lot in with the Mariel exodus; he wanted to find out about capitalism, what the monster they had portrayed was really like. In Miami he started to work in construction but he developed a taste for Coca-Cola, hamburgers, cars, blondes, going out and enjoying himself—he was attracted to the world over here. Work didn't give him enough to buy what he wanted, to go around town with rubies and a new car, so he ended up being asked to join a bank robbery. "It's very easy," they told him. "You go, take out your pistol, pass them a note that says, 'This is a stickup, give me the money from the safe.'"

So he did it and he scored twenty thousand dollars on his first go; the next time a little more money, and then he dedicated himself entirely to buying cars, motorcycles, clothes, drinks, and drugs. But since gringos are idiots, but not all of them are, one day he came out from a bank with his bag of bills and suddenly the bills began to emit a red dye in all directions. Betrayed. Up until then it was the American Way of Life. He was a very elegant Cuban who ended up in the Dog House because in Memphis he'd become a drug dealer. It's obvious that it's the Colombians who bring the little bird to the United States, but those who deal it and make the money that we ourselves never make are the Cubans. Where there are drugs, as they say around here, there's a Marielito selling it.

After two years they transferred me to a third-level cellblock on account of my good conduct. There you could work making fiber-optic cables for NASA or uniforms for the army. I was piling up time that went toward asking for release on parole. In the afternoon I played chess with a big guy, ruddy-faced and very gentle, who never spoke a word to me because he didn't know English. He was probably Polish, and during the two years I won some twenty-five matches. We became great friends and we rewarded each other with smiles, handshakes, and, at times, even the apples that they gave us for lunch. One afternoon, however, he didn't show up, and later I learned from the television that he had been exchanged for twenty-five Western spies, five gringos, ten English, and ten who knows what. He was an atomic expert. ▓

When I got out on parole, Mi Gente was standing in the door of the penitentiary waiting for me. Happy, I kissed him because after so much coldness you need to be loved. We went directly to have a drink in the first bar we found, and when we left we kept drinking in his apartment and laying out coke like madmen. The place was filling up with Colombians of all classes. From mules to the tough guys who transport it from San Francisco or take it to New York; from those who sell it to them to those who condemn the Cubans for being turncoats. There was a war in South Beach between the Colombians and the Cubans that cost forty lives and millions of dollars.

On my third day free, Mi Gente said to me that he was coming up with a plan of escape so I could earn my money the legal way. I had thought that making money decently wasn't completely impossible and that, if I could picture myself with the beasts behind bars, why couldn't I also picture myself with those who know how to make their money and enjoy it? Respecting the rules of the legal game was, in any case, easier than playing cards with the tough guys. Mi Gente helped me to make the decision and found me a part-time job washing cars in a car wash, but when I had finished my parole, he told me, "Man, I'd have thought that what would work for you is to work in what you know, because you're not going to become a doctor or an engineer or a priest. What you know how to do is to work with fear—all right then, go work with a retired colonel, a friend of mine—we've been close for a long time. He's put together a security firm to protect banks, residences, buildings. Shoemaker, back to your shoes! Do it, brother. The man asked me for a head of security to keep a handle on all those difficult dudes that he's hiring as bodyguards and escorts to take care of rich people and VIPs. He needs a hardworking partner, so, while we were talking, I told him that you were perfect."

And so it was. The job worked out. I started to work with twenty men, all of them ex-military men that my partner, the colonel, had under his command: lieutenants, sergeants, corporals. It was a simple affair: signing papers at a notary, permits for the weapons, guns and a license to do business from the Ministry of Defense. We started by guarding a closed warehouse north of Bogotá, then with two and later three, and after six months I had made my first million without suffering a toothache. Earning it this way was much easier. Within a year we were guarding jewelry stores, buildings, and warehouses. My colonel received offers every day. He managed the business affairs and I managed the business. I put my men in uniforms that made them look like Miami policemen, to give our clients more security. That idea made us rich. The secret was in our discipline and in the image we projected.

Going the legal route has the advantage of helping you grow old without noticing it. You become a mere administrator of your own life. You don't have to let your life stray from the track where it runs while you go about turning white and dying without anxiety or fear of the end. I can say all that now because I am so far from evil and so close to good.

Notes

Each chapter relates the story of a different Colombian caught up in the drug trade. Most are in jail, doing time, when they are narrating their story. The time frame varies from the late 1960s to the 1990s.

From the Maelstrom, with Their Country on Their Backs

1. I am indebted to Paul Wolf, not only for his regular updates on the developing situation in Colombia today but also for his work on uncovering Colombia's recent history. See www.derechos.net/paulwolf.

2. Andrés López-Restrepo and Alvaro Camacho-Guizado, *From Smuggler to Drug-Lords to "Traquetos": Changes in the Colombian Illicit Drug Organizations.* Available at http://www.nd.edu/~kellogg/pdfs/LopeCama.pdf. Also see Andrés López-Restrepo, "De la prohibición a la guerra: El narcotráfico colombiano en el siglo XX," in *Cambio de siglo—Balances y perspectivas* (Bogotá: IEPRI, 2000).

3. Roque Dalton, *Miguel Marmol*, trans. Kathleen Ross and Richard Schaaf (Willimantic, Conn.: Curbstone, 1987).

The Mule Driver

1. DAS (Departamento Administrativo de Seguridad) is Colombia's secret police.

2. The mules swallow a plastic or rubber container about the size of a narrow brownie. Condoms are sometimes used to hold the cocaine, and, as noted in the text, the mules must swallow and hold down as many as forty or fifty containers for twenty-four hours or longer.

3. To be *coronado* (from *coronar*) is to make your shipment successfully and get paid. It carries with it the sense of being a winner, pulling off a tough assignment, and is used throughout this book by people in the drug trade.

4. Plaza de Castilla to Carabanchel: from the police station to prison. Carabanchel is located on the outskirts of Madrid but is now shut down.

5. Parakeet, little bird, girl, snow: all knicknames for cocaine that exist in both English and Spanish. Horse, of course, is heroin.

6. El Tigre: The Tiger. In Spanish jails the bathroom—where prisoners can settle their disputes out of sight of the guards.

Scuzzball

1. To make *pasta, basa, paste,* or *base* (Cocaine sulphate), coca leaves are stripped from the plant. They are put into a plastic pit with a solution of water

and dilute sulphuric acid. A barefoot man will climb into the pit, walk on the mess; and shove it around with his hands. The goal is, after drying, to have the same, or greater, weight of material left over as when you started (hence the percentages). In South America coca paste is commonly mixed with tobacco and smoked. *Basuco* is impure cocaine in a dried form.

2. The Leopards are Colombia's special narcotics police. The DEA is, of course, the U.S. Drug Enforcement Administration, which is heavily involved in drug efforts throughout Latin America, but especially in Colombia at the present time. Their record of perpetual failure and social mayhem has never impeded steady increases in funding.

Hanged Man

1. Based on the account given in this chapter, it appears that Roberto Gaviria and Pablo Escobar, two men who would later make their fortunes and become notorious as heads of cocaine cartels, started out as bicycle thieves and headstone robbers.

2. Boca Junior is the complex of sports stadiums and parks in Buenos Aires, Argentina. The assertion that Evita Perón was really Colombian is fanciful.

Eight Years, Three Months, One Day

1. "Yesterday's Waves": "Espumas que se van," a popular Colombian pasillo by Jorge Villamil.

2. Luis Roldán Ibáñez, from his appointment as director general of the Spanish Guardia Civil in November 1986 until his arrest in December 1993, operated a one-man crime wave from his office, embezzling government money. He went to prison, escaped to Asia, was recaptured, and is currently Spain's wealthiest and most expensive prisoner. www.udel.edu/leipzig/texts4/elg27028.htm.

3. Yeserias, Envigado: Spanish prisons.

4. San Quintin: to go straight to the prison authorities.

5. "Without breakfast": totally clueless, with nothing to go on.

6. El Tigre: see note 6, chapter 1.

Sharon's Diary

1. *Marimba:* slang for marijuana. In many dictionaries the word that immediately follows marijuana.

2. Cacha, Perla, Aguadija: literally, Crooked (or Horny), Pearl, Runny.

3. *Macha:* macho woman; *cacha:* see note 2, this chapter; *tacha:* fault or defect, also a large tack, a pain in the ass.

4. *Maracachafa:* another slang term for marijuana.

5. "Ojitos Tapatíos," a folksong from north central Mexico, near Guadalajara.

6. This account confuses the Mona Channel—between the Dominican Republic and Puerto Rico—with the Windward Passage—between Cuba and Haiti, where there are likely to be Cuban ships watching out for potential es-

capees from the Castro regime. The Mona Channel is well known by Dominican exiles for its tricky currents and rapidly shifting weather but is more closely watched by the American coast guard looking for illegal immigrants from the DR. This error is repeated several times in the chapter.

7. Vallenatos: a style of music popular in Colombia.

8. *Desaguadero:* literally, Drain, as in drain pipe, i.e., the pits, middle of nowhere.

9. *Pisco:* the cane rum of the Andes.

The Nun

1. *Chicha* is the corn beer popular in the Andes region.

2. The Salt Cathedral at Zipaquirá took five years to build (1991–1996) and is housed within an existing salt mine. The site of the cathedral dates back to the Muisca Indians. The cathedral is located 390 feet below ground level and covers an area of 26,250 square feet. Built by Roswell Garavito Pearl, it took 250,000 tons of salt just to build the columns and lofts. http://www.catedraldesal.com/.

3. Pesetas, the old Spanish currency, were replaced by the Euro in January 2000.

4. The reference is to the Hawaiian island where for many years there was a leper colony run by Father Damian de Veuster, who ended up becoming a leper himself.

5. The attack comes not from taking heroin but from not taking it: what the Spaniards call the "monkey bitch," we call cold turkey.

6. *La Violencia,* rendered here as civil war, is the name Colombians give to the thus far unending stalemate between the government and the guerrillas that broke out in the 1940s after the assassination of the labor leader and presidential hopeful Gaitán.

Puppet

This chapter begins in Colombia in the early 1970s.

1. *Maracachafa:* see note 4, chapter 5.

2. Amazonas is Colombia's southernmost state. Leticia is located in a small finger of Colombian territory where Colombia, Peru, and Brazil meet, a well-known frontier area where lawlessness abounds—cf. the nun's account in chapter 6.

3. "Mejor mujer y media que media mujer" in the original.

4. F-2: Part of Colombian state security, one of the organizations in charge of cleaning up crime in the cities.

5. *Basuco* is sold in powder form and is consumed with a pinch of tobacco or marijuana; its effect lasts four or five minutes for each cigarette.

6. In 1980 approximately 125,000 Cubans—a great number of hardcore criminals but also gays, political dissidents, mentally disturbed people, and others—

left their country on rafts and boats for the coasts of southern Florida in what is known as the Mariel exodus (hence the term *Marielito*). The writer Reinaldo Arenas was one of them, and so was this communist, who evidently wanted to know what the U.S. was really like.

7. *Worm* is the term used by Cubans in Cuba to denote those who have fled the island, for whatever reason.